Americans Abroad

A Comparative Study of
Emigrants from the
United States

ENVIRONMENT, DEVELOPMENT, AND PUBLIC POLICY

A series of volumes under the general editorship of
Lawrence Susskind, *Massachusetts Institute of Technology,
Cambridge, Massachusetts*

PUBLIC POLICY AND SOCIAL SERVICES

Series Editor: Gary Marx, *Massachusetts Institute of Technology,
Cambridge, Massachusetts*

Recent Volumes in this Series

Other subseries:

ENVIRONMENTAL POLICY AND PLANNING

Series Editor: Lawrence Susskind, *Massachusetts Institute of Technology,
Cambridge, Massachusetts*

CITIES AND DEVELOPMENT

Series Editor: Lloyd Rodwin, *Massachusetts Institute of Technology,
Cambridge, Massachusetts*

Americans Abroad
A Comparative Study of Emigrants from the United States

Arnold Dashefsky
University of Connecticut
Storrs, Connecticut

Jan DeAmicis
Utica College
Utica, New York

Bernard Lazerwitz
and
Ephraim Tabory
Bar Ilan University
Ramat Gan, Israel

Plenum Press • New York and London

Library of Congress Cataloging-in-Publication Data

Americans abroad : a comparative study of emigrants from the United
  States / Arnold Dashefsky ... [et al.].
       p.   cm. -- (Environment, development, and public policy.
  Public policy and social services)
    Includes bibliographical references and index.
    ISBN 0-306-43941-7
    1. Americans--Foreign countries--Psychology. 2. United States-
  -Emigration and immigration--Psychological aspects.   I. Dashefsky,
  Arnold.   II. Series.
  E184.2.A44 1991
  304.8'0973--dc20   91-34502
                                                                CIP

ISBN 0-306-43941-7

© 1992 Plenum Press, New York
A Division of Plenum Publishing Corporation
233 Spring Street, New York, N.Y. 10013

Printed in the United States of America

Preface

An American college student traveling around Europe on a bicycle with two friends arrived at a recent July 4th celebration in Moscow and remarked, "We've been traveling around Europe and Russia for almost a month now. I never thought I'd be saying this, but I never wanted to see and hear Americans so much in my life. That would be so corny back home. But here it just seems right" (*Hartford Courant*, July 5, 1989, p. A2). Apparently you can take an American out of America, but you cannot take America out of an American—and perhaps this notion applies to other migrants as well.

This is a book that explores the experience of Americans abroad, specifically those who are living in other countries of the developed world with a lower standard of living than that of the United States. This study compares the travels and travails of emigrants to Australia and Israel and seeks to apply a social psychological perspective to address three questions: (1) What accounts for the motivation of migrants to move? (2) What are the sources of the adjustment problems the migrants experience? (3) What explains whether the migrants remain or return to the United States?

Ideally, it would be best to devise one instrument to gather data on representative samples of Americans living in a variety of countries abroad, but such an effort is beyond the resources of most researchers—including us. Therefore, we embraced the next best strategy: to compare the experience of Americans in two countries in the developed world for which we had data—Australia and Israel, two of the leading recipients of U.S. emigrants.

Chapter 1 develops a social psychological approach to the study of emigration as a particular aspect of the literature on international migration. Chapter 2 presents an approach to understanding emigration derived from the work of the classical sociologist Emile Durkheim and reviews the data sources and methods for the study. In Chapters 3–4, we offer an answer to the first question on motivation. In Chapter 5, we examine the second question by reporting the adaptations and adjustments of the immigrants to their host society. Chapter 6 begins to provide the reader with an answer to the third question by comparing Australian and Israeli differences and similarities with respect to staying in the host country or returning home, including a "model of the migration cycle." Chapter 7 concludes the presentation of our findings with respect to the third question by examining the factors involved in the decision to remain or return home. Finally, Chapter 8 includes a summary of the findings as well as the theoretical, research, and social implications of our study.

While there have been many studies of migrants, they typically focus on the experience of a group of immigrants moving from one country with a lower standard of living to a new society with a higher living standard, such as the United States. Our study is distinctive in that it offers a comparative analysis of the equivalent experience of Americans as emigrants in adapting to two different countries, Australia and Israel, both with a lower standard of living. Along these lines, our study furthermore contributes to a broader understanding of emigration in the following ways:

1. We treat emigration theoretically as a cyclical rather than static process. This is through our analysis of motivations, adjustments, and return migration. Also, we suggest that people in particular "creases" or loosely integrated stages in their life cycle are more prone to migrate.
2. By examining the behavior of Americans abroad, we reveal core aspects of American culture: the centrality of productivity and efficiency in work; the importance of equal status in issues of gender; the continued existence of a spirit of adventure and pioneering challenge; and the strong appreciation of American culture, resulting in a great reluctance to give up American citizenship.
3. Finally, we highlight a finding that belongs more to the "sociology of sociology": that the ratio of studies of emigration to immigration in recent American social science literature has been about 1:7, whereas the proportion of actual emigration to immigration in the twentieth century in the United States has been more than twice as great at about 1:3. Even within the social sciences, the concern with America as a recipient of immigrants has masked the level at which it also produces emigrants— those who do not validate the predominant assumption of the virtue of this society by their ultimate integration.

The British author Salman Rushdie, born in Bombay to a Muslim family that later moved to Karachi, has experienced the unusual problems of the emigrants. Indeed, his book *The Satanic Verses*, which has earned him the death sentence in absentia by Iran's ruling clergy, deals with the issue of multiple identities. As Rushdie stated, "And what I am saying to you—and saying in the novel—is that we have got to come to terms with this. We are increasingly becoming a world of migrants, made up of bits and fragments from here, there. We are here. And we have never really left anywhere we have been" (*New York Times*, February 23, 1990, p. C18). Atypical as the emigrant experience appears to late-twentieth-century citizens of the United States, it may foreshadow a more popular trend for the twenty-first-century citizens of the world.

Acknowledgments

The idea for a book on the topic of American emigration originated with a grant that Arnold Dashefsky and Bernard Lazerwitz received in 1981 from the American Sociological Association's "Committee on Problems of the Discipline." This committee, composed of Immanuel Wallerstein, Norman Birnbaum, Hubert M. Blalock, Morris Rosenberg, and Russell R. Dynes, made awards at that time to support conferences aimed at promoting three underdeveloped lines of inquiry in sociology. Our conference was convened in the late summer of 1982 with most of the sessions held at the University of Connecticut in Storrs. Another session was organized in conjunction with the 1982 Annual Meeting of the American Sociological Association in Toronto.

Several colleagues joined us for one or more of these sessions of the conference, whose objectives were to clarify the relationship between alienation and emigration, explain the dynamics of return migration, and seek new integration of data sources on American emigrants. Ultimately, through the course of subsequent study, we learned that alienation was less important in explaining emigration than originally thought; that return migration was not necessarily the end of the migration experience; and that the integration of data on emigrants could be accomplished through further research and the preparation of this book.

One disappointment resulting from the conference and our subsequent investigations was the paucity of data available on Americans abroad. Perhaps only Americans are interested in American emigrants. Once abroad, however, these immigrants are of no greater interest than other migrants and retrieving separate data on them is, understandably, not particularly illuminating to foreign authorities.

The initiation of the conference led Jan DeAmicis to communicate an interest in this topic based on his research on American emigrants in Australia done several years earlier. This collaboration led to a paper by Dashefsky, DeAmicis, and Lazerwitz on American emigrants, which was presented at the 1983 Annual

Meeting of the American Sociological Association and subsequently published in *Comparative Sociological Review* (1984). The success of that effort encouraged further collaboration, which ultimately resulted in this book.

Over the span of nearly two decades, Ephraim Tabory has been an integral part of this effort—first in interviewing Americans in Israel, and later parents of North American migrants, to provide a more total picture of American emigrants. Therefore, it was most useful that he joined our collaborative effort.

Each of us has been engaged in thinking, researching, and writing about this topic intermittently but consistently for nearly two decades. Such a long period of involvement, of course, requires the assistance of many individuals and organizations. In addition to the American Sociological Association, whose grant we acknowledged above, we would like to thank the University of Connecticut for granting sabbatical leave to Arnold Dashefsky, and its Research Foundation for providing funds to support the research effort in its various stages. In addition, thanks are due the Bar Ilan University Research Committee for providing funds to procure data on Americans in Israel and for granting sabbatical leave and travel grant support to Bernard Lazerwitz and Ephraim Tabory to aid in this collaborative effort. Thanks are also due Utica College for its support of this project, including travel grants to Jan DeAmicis to collaborate on this research. Special thanks go to Maureen Scoones and Joe Paxhia for their help with the Australian data.

In the course of conducting the original research, each of us received much support from a variety of agencies and individuals. With regard to the acquisition and analysis of the Israeli data, we wish to thank the Israel Central Bureau of Statistics for access to the North American data of the Immigrant Absorption Survey. Of particular help in this regard were Moshe Sicron, Eitan Sabatello, Joseph Askenazi, and Avi Ackermann. Valuable research assistance was provided in Israel by Sarah Cohen. The funds for the first phase of this project were provided by the National Institute of Mental Health, United States Public Health Services, Grant No. IR03 MH 24072–01A1. In addition, thanks are also due to the Memorial Foundation for Jewish Culture and the National Endowment for Humanities Summer Stipend, both of which provided partial funding for this project.

Additional valuable research assistance in the United States was provided by Arlene Gottschalk, Dan Jansenson, Ann Mardenfield, Jeffrey Schwartz, Millie Spector, Linda Stark, Lynne Stein, Beth Troy, Mark Weinberg, David Wrubel, and Bill Zall. We are also grateful to the Association of Parents of North American Israelis, and particularly to Bernice Saltzman, for providing us with useful data on the parental experience of their children's emigration. Last but not least, the generous assistance of the Australian Department of Labour and Immigration and the Department of Social Security is gratefully acknowledged.

During the progress of our study, many colleagues provided helpful insights to aid in the course of the research and writing, including Mark Abrahamson, Alan Davidson, Ada Finifter, Bernard Finifter, Josef Gugler, Jerry Heiss, Dennison Nash, and Don Waldman. Series Editor Gary Marx has demonstrated much enthusiasm for our work and provided valuable critical comments to improve our manuscript; and, of course, Eliot Werner, Executive Editor at Plenum, displayed an indispensable confidence that we would complete this book in a timely fashion. To all of these individuals we are extremely grateful, but we assume responsibility for any errors herein.

The preparation of a lengthy manuscript requires the typing assistance of a person with an unusual amount of patience to endure the multiple revisions necessary when a work circulates among several authors. Carolee Tollefson is such a person and we are deeply in her debt. Thanks are also due to three undergraduate assistants, Martha Altieri, Christine Beardry, and Turissa Campbell, all of the University of Connecticut, who provided a variety of services to aid in the final preparation of the manuscript. Also, we would like to thank Debbie Crary and Carol Roberts of the University of Connecticut Research Foundation, who graciously assisted in making the manuscript for this book machine-readable. Finally, thanks are due Robert Freire of Plenum for his able assistance as Production Editor of this volume.

Last but certainly not least, we want to thank our families, who at one point or another shared the emigrant experience with us and supported us in our chosen research endeavor. Our warmest thanks go to our spouses (Sandy, Linda, Gertrude, and Mala) and to our children (Michael and Alisa; Justin; Elliot and Ellen; and Shlomit and Amiel).

In conclusion, we owe a debt of gratitude to all those respondents who participated in our research. Without their testimony, we would not be able to say anything. Our special thanks go to all of those American emigrants—and emigrants everywhere—who have dared to move to build a better way of life for themselves, their families, and their community.

Contents

1

International Migration

Sociological or Social Psychological Phenomenon?

Should some extraterrestrial creature arrive to study the habits and customs of the people of the United States, it would likely report that Americans are a restless people frequently on the move. Such mobility might be the cultural consequence of succeeding waves of foreign migration to its shores, from the first migrants—the native Americans—to the more recent streams of Asian, Latin, and Caribbean migrants, and it has taken many forms. For many of these migrants, America was symbolized by the Statue of Liberty beckoning with its beacon to the "tired . . . poor . . . (and) huddled masses." This international migration has been paralleled by an internal migration, which in the nineteenth century was associated with the development of the West and in the second half of the twentieth century takes the form of a Sunbelt migration.[1]

[1]With respect to internal migration, the decennial proportion of the native population who resided in one state but were born elsewhere has increased from 23% in 1870 to 32% in 1970. This means that in 1970, 62,157,632 of all native-born Americans were born outside the state in which they were residing compared to 7,669,802 Americans in 1870. While the native-born population had increased about sixfold between 1870 and 1970, the level of interstate migration had increased eightfold in the same period. Furthermore, between 1960 and 1970, California and Florida had the greatest amount of net intercensal migration of the 50 states (U.S. Bureau of the Census, 1975, pp. 87–93). In order to give some perspective, we sought to assess the relative amounts of international migration (immigration and emigration) and internal migration on an intercensal basis during the twentieth century in the United States. Based on Warren and Kraly (1985), the average amount of immigration between censuses from 1900 to 1980 was 3.75 million compared to 1.25 million for emigration. During approximately the same period, the average amount of internal migration between censuses from 1900 to 1970 was 31.75 million (U.S. Bureau of the Census, 1975, p. 89). In other words, on average the number of native-born persons in a census year in the twentieth century who were born in a different state than the one in which they were residing was 8.5 times greater than the number of immigrants and 25 times greater than the number of emigrants.

Indeed, the phenomenon of migration, in general, is fundamental to the understanding of the variety of human civilizations on this planet. Without the movement of human beings across the surface of the earth, we would likely be confined to some small piece of land between the horn of northeast Africa and the Arabian peninsula of western Asia, were we to have survived at all. In fact, this experience of migration is central to some of the earliest myths of Western civilization. In the story of Adam and Eve, God exiles them from the Garden of Eden for their transgression. Hence, migration is associated with the loss of paradise. Furthermore, in the succeeding biblical story of Cain and Abel, the farmer Cain is accused by God of the murder of his brother, the shepherd Abel; and his punishment is to become a "restless wanderer," a migrant.[2] No wonder Clifford Jansen (1969) has pointed out that human migration is nearly as old as the human species.

Despite the importance of migration for human beings, much of its history and prehistory lies buried in the outer crust of the earth. Such buried treasures are occasionally uncovered by archaeologists and others, which yield some clues to the history of migration. This study, however, will focus on one of the latest steps taken by human beings on the migratory path and will rely on the explanation of this phenomenon through social science surveys rather than excavation of archaeological artifacts.

MIGRATION AND INTERNATIONAL MIGRATION

In the growth and decline of population in society, three central variables are involved:

1. *fertility*, which is the measure of births in a population;
2. *mortality*, which is the measure of deaths in a population; and
3. *migration*, which is the measure of population movement in space.

Families may choose how many children they want in accordance with their religious beliefs, cultural norms, family situation, and perhaps even government incentives and negative sanctions. Rapid gains in medical knowledge have led to an extension of life and to changes in the causes of death. These factors affect the demographic distribution and composition *within* society. The third factor, migration, is especially interesting because we have much more control over our decision to move from one area to another than we do regarding our birth or death. Along these lines, Matras (1973, p. 360) has defined a *migrant* as a person

[2]This interpretation was suggested by Professor Eddy Zemach at a lecture at the University of Connecticut, February 27, 1989.

who moves into or out of a population by means other than birth or death, and *migration* is the total increase or decrease in the population associated with such movement.

One of the fundamental distinctions in the study of migration is between migration *within* countries (internal or intranational) and migration *between* countries (external or international). Some have argued that the causes and consequences of *internal* and *international* migration are the same, but Goldscheider (1971, p. 65) argues that the generally greater distances, cultural and linguistic obstacles, and legal and political barriers to international migration necessitate separate explanations for each phenomenon. International migration, therefore, produces more types and a greater amount of change than internal migration. These greater changes associated with international migration, according to Goldscheider (1971, p. 66), are due to "(1) distance covered, (2) impeding factors, (3) heterogeneity between the area of origin and the area of destination." In this way, Goldscheider has emphasized the centrality of the issues of changes associated with migration, that is, changes for the society and changes for individuals. The task of the student of migration is to explain the changes for society and for individuals that precipitate migration and that result from migration.

In particular, we are interested in this book in focusing on the level of migrating individuals within the context of the sending or receiving society rather than the societal level alone. Why do particular people leave their homes, travel to a foreign land, and decide to settle there? Why do they make their decisions to leave and how do they cope with the new culture? How well do they fit in and start new lives? Who returns to the "old world"? In particular, why do Americans do these things? By combining data from sample surveys, in-depth interviews, census data, and published research, we seek to answer why individual Americans move abroad.

Following Goldscheider's distinction (1971) stated above, this study will confine itself to an examination of the issue of American emigration since the 1960s within the context of international migration. In this regard, there have been two basic themes in seeking to explain migration: the first examines the various motives for migration; the second studies the degree to which migration motives are resolved by the act of migration and subsequent adjustment. In the first approach, the works of Eisenstadt (1954), Lee (1966), and Bogue (1969) are useful. For the second approach, the studies of Eisenstadt (1954) as well as Herman (1970), who based his work on the field theory of Lewin (1951), are relevant.[3]

---

[3]This literature represents a microfunctionalist (or configurationist) approach (associated with gestalt psychology, field theory, dissonance theory, balance theory, and so on). This "viewpoint argues that the human being is constantly driven to achieve an orderly and balanced grasp of the world derived from a 'gestalt'—a sudden insight or configuration of phenomena" that permits the individual "to function in social groups on the basis of the consistency achieved" (Dashefsky, 1976, p. 112).

What much of this literature has in common is a set of assumptions derived from demographic statistics and facts and functional analyses about sending and receiving societies. Typically, motives for migration are expressed as "pushes" and "pulls." People are driven from their homes by political oppression, economic chaos, or some other form of societal instability. They are "pulled" to a "land of opportunity," where disruptions of home are left behind, where they can make a new start in life. Most migration research focuses on large-scale movements of people: war refugees, victims of the Industrial Revolution, or people fleeing other societal disasters. "Brain drain" researchers point out the cost-benefit analysis that "pulls" the most ambitious and well-trained from lower to higher regions of economic opportunity, but without the "push" of imminent disaster. For most migration streams, such analysis has been appropriate and fruitful. But this mode of analysis does not easily explain the case of those Americans who move and settle abroad for a number of reasons.

First, most migration analysis is at the macrolevel and concentrates on large-scale streams linked to social systems and social institutions: the economy, polity, and so forth. Social structure is assumed to affect individuals in particular ways (as pushes or pulls). These smaller streams of Americans involve individuals, not large groups, and the link between social structure and the individual biography is not a fruitful method of explanation for these people.

Second, the larger American migration streams (e.g., to Canada, Australia, and Israel, in that order) do not include the most dispossessed or politically oppressed: almost no blacks, Hispanics, or Native Americans, for instance.

Implicit in this model is the functionalist assumption that society and the individual strive for equilibrium. Migrants who enter the new system have their equilibrium upset, and they upset the equilibrium of the society. Ultimately, in most cases they are absorbed and their equilibrium as well as that of society is restored. Such an approach, based on the assumption that society is characterized by a good deal of consensus as to the appropriate norms and values governing people's behaviors, tends to emphasize the need for individuals to change their behavior and assimilate to the new culture and social structure. Eisenstadt (1954), for example, reported on the absorption of low-status Afro-Asian Jews in postindependence Israel at a time when economic, political, and social stability were perceived as essential for survival in an emerging heterogeneous society. An alternative approach to intergroup relations, focusing on pluralism and the extent to which there is conflict and disagreement over the appropriate norms and values governing people's behavior, emerged in the 1960s (see Dashefsky, 1976). Because this perspective has been developed relatively recently, it might explain why Matras found such scant research conducted on the relative "success" of the migrant in the new society (1973, p. 380). There is a need to go beyond the emphasis on the perspective of the social system and the assumption that migrants of necessity must assimilate and adjust to the new society. We cannot assume that migrants have little alternative to such adjustment. We need to examine the ways they define themselves in their new societies. Applying the pluralism perspective permits one to consider the case of migrants who do not assimilate in the system as the functional model expects them to do (see Dashefsky and Lazerwitz, 1986). This point will be developed subsequently when we discuss American influences on Israeli society, especially on religious life.

Indeed, migrating Americans tend to be well-educated, white, young adults who have enormous economic opportunities at home.

Third, they tend to move as individuals or young couples (except for young children in family units) rather than as large social groups or geographic communities. Those who go to Australia, Canada, and Israel are drawn from all parts of America and in units rarely larger than the nuclear family. Thus, while migration research usually focuses on the group level, which is appropriate, of course, to the discipline of sociology, it is necessary to develop a microlevel explanation and focus on the individual as the unit of analysis. The study of migration needs more research into why particular individuals move.

Fourth, motives for moving should not be confused with motives for staying or returning. This is easiest to appreciate in the case of Americans who move to Australia. For example, in Australia we studied only those Americans who had Migrant Settler Visas. However, the majority claimed they had no intention of staying permanently at the time they moved. They did not really migrate as the term is widely understood. Nevertheless, many have stayed much longer than anticipated—sometimes 20 to 30 years—and still claim they might not stay for good! That is, they became settlers, and in a sense are still becoming settlers, for reasons very different from why they went in the first place.

Thus, we intend to investigate the migrants' reasons for going, for staying, and for returning. Their reasons are often highly personal and diverse, but there are patterns that are discernible. These patterns, however, are not easily identifiable from a social structural level of analysis. To fully uncover them, it is necessary to analyze the behavior of individuals. That is, we have tried to link biography to social structure by proceeding from data derived from the individuals, rather than by focusing on society and inferring individual motives. We intend to explain why these particular people moved, and this requires recognition of emotions, knowledge (often imperfect), identity, interpersonal relationships, and even "drift."

Our emphasis, therefore, is on voluntary international migrants who have the possibility of returning home. As Beijer (1969, p. 39) has pointed out, they have received little scholarly attention. Such voluntary international migration is frequently ideologically motivated, but only infrequently do scholars note this. Petersen (1975) defines this group as "free" migrants. They are characterized by a small-scale movement of pioneers who are estranged and have drifted apart from their home society. Such voluntary international migration represents an estimated 5 to 7 percent of the total international migration since 1945 (Beijer, 1969, p. 23). Indeed, the United States has been an important destination for many of these migrants.

Despite the flow of immigrants coming to American shores, there has generally been an ebb of migrants leaving. In the twentieth century hundreds of thousands of Americans have left to settle elsewhere. According to Warren and

Kraly (1985, p. 5), 789,000 U.S. citizens have emigrated in the period 1900–1979. Indeed, it is a subject not frequently studied systematically, perhaps because of the ideological bias favoring the view of America as the great "melting pot" which sociologists recently have suggested is less factual than fanciful a notion (Newman, 1973; Dashefsky, 1976; Alba and Chamlin, 1983).[4] In fact, Warren and Kraly (1985, p. 5) have reported that the number of emigrants leaving the United States between 1900 and 1979 represented approximately one third the number of all immigrants.[5]

We know quite a bit about those who stayed. Indeed, one of the first major American empirical studies in sociology was Thomas and Znaniecki's analysis of Polish immigrants in Chicago (1920). On the other hand, we know very little about those who returned to the Old Country or migrated elsewhere. Similarly, we know very little about those native "homegrown" Americans who have emigrated abroad. Our best explanations postulate alienation, or ideology, or frontier restlessness. Are these satisfying explanations?

Systematic study reveals that they are not sufficient. As we have noted, these are individuals, and not "populations," and our traditional models do not work well. We need individual-rooted explanations to account for those who move abroad and stay.

SOCIOLOGICAL VERSUS SOCIAL PSYCHOLOGICAL EXPLANATIONS

Just as international migration is a phenomenon that knows few political boundaries, so too it knows few disciplinary boundaries. It has been difficult, therefore, to construct a general theory of migration. Jansen has summarized the scope of the explanations of migration that exist:

> Migration is a demographic problem: It influences sizes of population at origin and destination; it is an economic problem: a majority of shifts in population are due to economic imbalances between areas; it may be a political problem: this is particularly so in international migrations where restrictions and conditions apply to those wishing to cross a political boundary; it involves social psychology in so far as the migrant is involved in a process of decision-making before moving and that his personality may play an important role in the success with which he integrates into the host society; it is also a sociological problem since the social structure and cultural system both of places of origin and of destination are affected by migration and in turn affect the migrant. (1969, p. 60)

[4]Parts of the preceding section are derived from Dashefsky, DeAmicis, and Lazerwitz (1984).
[5]According to the United Nations (1978, p. 534), the term "emigrant" refers to "residents intending to remain for a period of more than one year." In fact, the UN (1978, p. 56) acknowledges that this concept is subject to varying international interpretations.

The particular difficulty of constructing a theoretical model of migration has been attributed by Jackson to the central role of the migrant in sociological analyses:

> Just as he is often seen as a threat to the society he leaves (brain drain, etc.) and a threat to the society to which he comes, he presents for the sociologist a serious challenge to any restricted and narrowly functional or static model of human society. The migrant not only provides the human capital of social changes, he is its agent and as such he plays a significant part in shaping ideas about the society in which he lives. (1969, p. 8)

The major weakness of the migration literature is the failure to really explain why individuals move. The reason for this is that most students of migration look at migration from either a sociohistorical level or sociological level. Thus, migration is explained in terms of extraordinary events, such as economic dislocation, political repression, and religious persecution. This kind of explanation only takes us so far in that it does not tell us how these broad sociocultural factors impinge on individuals and transform them into migrants. For example, we are familiar with the stories of early English migration to America: of the Pilgrims who sought to build a New World free to practice their religious beliefs, or William Penn and the Quakers who also sought religious freedom, and of the debtors released from prison who settled in Georgia. These migrants came primarily to seek a fresh start in life free of economic handicaps and religious restrictions. But which Pilgrims came to "Plimoth Plantation," and which Quakers came to "Penn's Woods" (Pennsylvania), and which debtors arrived in Georgia? Similarly we may ask which Americans went to and stayed in Australia or Israel?

Of course, we are not the first to observe this general weakness in the sociological literature. Homans (1964), for example, took the functionalists to task for failing to really account for the actions of individuals in their attempted explanations of systems of behavior. Ultimately Homans argued that any satisfactory theory or explanation of human behavior had to bring people into the picture and not just names, roles, institutions, equilibrium systems, and so forth. As Homans stated:

> I now suspect that there are no general sociological propositions, propositions that hold good of all societies or social groups, as such, and that the only general propositions are in fact psychological. (1964, p. 817)

It is our contention that Homans' suggestion to rely only on psychological factors is too reductionist, just as sociological explanations are too general. Our approach is to focus on the individual in the hope of specifying more accurately the dynamics of migration—to build a social psychological explanation of migration.

Previous social psychological research has focused on the functionalist-inspired push-pull approach. According to Bogue:

> every departure for a new community . . . is either a response to some impelling need that the person believes he cannot satisfy in his present residence or a flight from a situation that for some reason has become undesirable, unpleasant, or intolerable. (1969, p. 753)

Where the destination exerts a pull on the migrant, the migration is a search for an opportunity to improve one's life. However, migration may also be caused by a flight from undesirable social or economic conditions which represents a push.

Bogue (1961, p. 13) further noted that both these factors may operate simultaneously in the migration process. In such a case, push factors are those causing people to leave their area of origin and pull factors are those attracting them to a particular alternative.

Lee (1966, p. 50) argued that there are four factors associated with the decision and act of voluntary migration:

1. Those associated with the area of origin.
2. Those associated with the area of destination.
3. Intervening obstacles.
4. Personal factors.

Furthemore, Lee noted that potential migrants usually have a deeper and longer-term acquaintance with their current area of residence and are able to view it in a considered and unhurried manner. There is usually more ignorance or mystery about the area of destination. The balance in favor of a move must be sufficient to overcome a natural inertia (that is, the total positive attraction of the area of destination must be greater than the attraction of remaining in the area of origin). Between every two points there is a set of obstacles. These may be distance, immigration laws, costs, and so on. Rossi (1955, p. 89), for example, found in a study of West Philadelphia that two out of three dissatisfied movers had been living in rented apartments, whereas only one third of the dissatisfied who did not move rented their homes. The burden of home ownership served as an intervening variable limiting one's ability to migrate freely. Finally, there are personal factors, such as personality, intelligence, age, and sex, affecting the decision to migrate.

Lee's model can be further understood by referring to Kurt Lewin's field theory. Lewin (1951, p. 239ff.) wrote of the individual's "life space," which consisted of the actor and the psychological environment as it exists for him or her. Life space is differentiated into regions, examples of which are family, social relations, emotions, and actions. "Behavior" is any change in the life space and is coordinated with the movement of the person in the life space (Lewin, 1951, p. 48).

The most important mode of behavior in the life space is locomotion, which may either be physical or psychological (Lewin, 1936, p. 47). Locomotion is produced by a "need" that corresponds to a tension in a certain system within the person. If two regions in the life space are in communication with each other and a need is aroused in one of them, "the tension is released if the goal is reached." In other words, locomotion from one region to the other takes place until a state of equilibrium is reached (Lewin, 1951, p. 9).

Lewin (1951, p. 257) designated the construct "force" as that which causes change, and he calls the effective force determining behavior the "resultant force," or the combination of the individual relevant forces. A particular region in the life space may be attractive for the person, in which case it is said to have a positive valence, or unattractive, and hence be of negative valence. Using Lewin's terminology, Lee's scheme for the area of destination and present residence may be explained as follows: There are various forces, some positive and some negative, affecting each of the regions. In a case of push, the more relevant goal region is the area of origin which has a negative valence and forces are producing locomotion away from that area. In a case of pull, the area of destination is seen as having positive valence and forces are producing locomotion toward the goal region.

Lee's intervening obstacles correspond to what Lewin (1951, p. 259) calls "restraining forces." Any locomotion, toward or away from a goal, may be hindered by some physical or social barriers. These restraining forces do not lead to locomotion, but they do influence the effect of the driving forces.

In the past, one could logically argue that the greater the distance between the area of origin and the area of destination, the greater the number of obstacles to be encountered. Stouffer (1940, p. 846), therefore, proposed that "the number of persons going a given distance is directly proportional to the number of opportunities at that distance and inversely proportional to the number of intervening opportunities." Once an area that reduces the tension has been reached, further migration should cease. In fact, distance per se is less important today than it once was given the ease of jet travel. One does not encounter "intervening cities" when one embarks on a nonstop plane.

While Lee differentiated between intervening variables and personal factors, Lewin stated that these are related, just as the perception of driving forces is inextricably related with a particular perceiver:

> The restraining forces, just as the driving forces, are due to a relation between two regions of the life space, namely, the nature of the barrier region, and the "ability" of the individual. The same social or physical obstacle corresponds, therefore, to different restraining forces for different individuals. (1951, p. 260)

Utilizing these concepts, then, Eisenstadt (1954) studied the migration of Afro-Asian Jews to Israel. He emphasized that every migration involves individuals whose tensions are aroused because of a negative force in the area of origin. This gives rise to a push to leave that area and settle in an area where the forces return to a balanced state. Herman (1970), also working in this tradition, examined the reactions of American undergraduates to their spending a year of study in Israel utilizing a positive-negative valence model.

The theories mentioned thus far refer to the individual's personal motivations. Petersen (1970, p. 523) has suggested a classification that considers both the migrant's personal motives as well as the broader social causes of migration. His system differentiates between a migrant whose purpose is to maintain existing conditions that may be threatened (conservative migration) and one who is seeking a change for the new (innovative migration). As Petersen explains, while an individual's motive may be either conservative or innovative, the force behind a particular migratory movement may vary. A state's policy, for example, may be to impel or force geographic relocation. In such a case it is possible that the government's policy of encouraging migration may be utilized by those seeking innovative change as well as by those who migrate to retain their former lifestyle. In other words, the necessity to move may be exploited by some as an opportunity to improve their former life situations while others may seek only to establish themselves in a location where they can preserve what they had previously had.

These approaches have been helpful in focusing on the individual within his or her immediate social environment as a means of explaining migration. Nevertheless, they largely fail to take into account the socialization experiences that shape the development of the individual (see Dashefsky, 1976, p. 143). Moreover, the broader social structural and cultural matrix in which the individual is enmeshed is likely to affect the decision to migrate. Such characteristics might include the roles and conceptions individuals perceive for themselves in society, the cultural values they espouse, the estrangement they experience in society, the structural opportunities they perceive or enjoy, and their interpersonal relationships.

Simply stated, the disadvantage of the push-pull model in migration is that it is too deterministic. It relies on a simple economic model depicting the potential migrant as a rational calculator of the negative and positive features of the areas of emigration and immigration. The inadequacy of the model is easily observed by noting that the majority of the world's population do not migrate even though the model would predict that many persons would be better off if they moved elsewhere. Apparently not everyone is calculating the same way.

A more elaborate social psychological model that might be of help in predicting migration has been put forth by Ajzen and Fishbein (1980). This model relates attitudes to behavior by noting that cognitions inform attitudes, and

attitudes affect behavior. One might decide to move, for example, when a particular set of cognitions relevant to the migration process are called into play.
Cognitions refer to the beliefs, impressions, and ideas that one has about a
particular object. One may feel that one's neighborhood enjoys a rainy climate, is
relatively safe, and very quiet. The sanitation system may be considered to be
insufficient. The neighbors may be seen as being remote. The school system may
be seen as being conservative. Junk food stores may be seen to be seriously
lacking. All of these are cognitions that may affect how satisfied one is with the
community. The cognitions can carry with them a positive or negative feeling, or
affect. While some people may like a rainy climate, others might prefer a hot and
humid area. Some parents may prefer traditional schools, while others prefer an
open school system. How important these cognitions are to individuals and their
particular evaluation of all the relevant cognitions can be combined to form an
overall attitude regarding the neighborhood or community.

According to this model, the resultant attitude leads to behavioral intentions. Intentions mean that all other factors being equal, a person will act in
accordance with his or her attitudes. The determining factor, though, is specified
in this model. It is that social norms or pressure may intervene and lead a person
to act contrary to his or her intentions. The classic case is the bigot who acts in a
civil manner to the person he or she does not like on a crowded street because of
the social norms that dictate civil behavior. Applied to the migration process, a
person may refuse to move and leave loved ones despite the fact that he or she
would be better off elsewhere. Family relationships may mean more than an
objective consideration of the benefits of migration.

This model is also insufficient for our needs. It does not explain why certain
cognitions are more important than others. Why are some people more sensitive
to some cognitive elements than other people? In other words, why are some
factors more salient for some people than for others? The socialization process,
meaning the manner in which the person was raised, surely has an impact here.
This experience sensitizes certain persons to their social environment and makes
particular individuals aware of contrasts that others, with different backgrounds,
do not feel. This is what is meant by a social psychological model—the impact
of social factors on the behavior of individuals.

Of particular interest in this study is the way in which the cognitions that
were relevant to the initial migration process change over time. One question that
we ask is whether the same set of factors that were initially involved in the
decision to move continue to be important once the move has been made. Will a
migrant be satisfied when the initial cognitions are fulfilled (or disappointed
when they are not), or do a new set of cognitions come into play once the
migration decision has been carried out.

This study, therefore, will seek to answer several social psychological questions within the context of American migration in the hope of enlarging our

understanding of the issue of migration. These answers will apply at least to the voluntaristic type of international migration that is oriented toward ideology, personal fulfillment, or family relationships. The significance of this phenomenon is that it will likely characterize an increasing proportion of migrants who migrate internally, as well as those who migrate internationally among industrialized societies that are compatible and homogeneous with respect to major institutions and cultures. This appears likely as the standard of living and socioeconomic status of much of the world's population rise and geographic mobility and migration on a voluntary, as opposed to coercive, basis become more possible. Perhaps people in the twenty-first century will be more able to choose whether they want to move to Washington or Warsaw, to Alaska or Australia, to California or Canada, or to Idaho or Israel. Furthermore, voluntaristic migrants might well decide to return home or move elsewhere, or decide to stay. Thus, the migrant may become transformed into a permanent settler, regardless of the original purpose of moving. We need to understand this process of transformation. Do they stop being Americans after living abroad for many years? Do they assimilate well enough to "pass for native" and is that important to them? Finally, do they surrender their earlier political loyalties? These are all questions begging for answers.

It is the primary objective of this study, therefore, to explore comparatively the phenomenon of the international migration of adult Americans within the developed world, emphasizing social psychological explanations. This study will investigate the motivations for migration, absorption in the host country, and the factors in return migration to the United States.

SUMMARY

Human migration appears to be nearly as old as the human species. It is one of the three central variables (along with fertility and mortality) that affect the increase or decrease of a population. *Migration* refers to the total increase or decrease in the population associated with the movement of individuals (migrants) into or out of a population by means other than birth or death. This study confines itself to the topic of *international migration*, or the migration between countries, as opposed to *internal migration* (within countries), for which separate explanations are needed.

Americans, in particular, who move abroad are interesting. They move from a country of legendary high standards of living, a country that has historically experienced an enormous influx of migrants. A nation of immigrants, the United States is not a traditional "sending nation" with a clear, steady stream of out-migration. Different types of Americans move to Australia and Israel; perhaps different types move to Canada as well. Who are they? Pioneers? Alienated

Americans? While our empirical knowledge is limited, there has been much speculation on this topic. The myth of the Alienated Americans, for example, has been a popular notion for explaining why they were migrating to Australia. Clearly theirs is not a hardship-induced migration, and few complain of harsh political or religious oppression (estrangement, perhaps, but not persecution). Leaving such a wealthy land, they are often economically secure and not seeking a fortune elsewhere. While there is a substantial literature on *immigration* to the United States, no model that we can find successfully explains American *emigration*.

Most themes in the international migration literature relate either to the investigation of the *motivations for migration* or the degree to which such motives are resolved by the subsequent *adjustment and absorption*. While most studies rarely examine both dimensions, it is our contention that both factors need to be dealt with in understanding the migration process, and we will consequently do so. In addition, a third dimension, the *factors in return migration* to the United States, will also be probed. Such an analysis is not only interesting in its own right, but also because it further illuminates the first two factors.

Moreover, our approach will emphasize *social psychological* (as opposed to sociological explanations) focusing on the *socialization and social interaction experiences* of the migrants.

In sum the questions to be answered in this study are:

1. What accounts for the motivations of migrants to move?
2. What are the sources of the adjustment problems the migrants experience?
3. What explains whether the migrants remain or return?

2

American Emigration

Past and Present

If there is one place in the United States by which Americans generally like to think the rest of the world's people regard them, it is the Statue of Liberty standing in New York harbor holding her torch aloft as a beacon signaling the new haven for the homeless and oppressed. (One sociologist has suggested that the second symbol of America abroad is the wagon train, which further illustrates the importance of migration in American culture.) Millions of immigrants passed in her shadow from the latter part of the nineteenth through the middle of the twentieth century. It is ironic that in the wake of the centennial celebration of the "Lady," or Statue of Liberty, it is now possible to examine in some detail the emigration of Americans abroad.

It is generally believed in the United States that while people abroad want to immigrate to America, Americans themselves do not wish to emigrate. While it may not be a startling revelation that some immigrants to these shores eventually return home, a new phenomenon has emerged in that an increasing number of native-born U.S. citizens are also emigrating.

Warren and Kraly have summarized the situation best:

> In a society founded on the assumption of individual freedom, the ability to leave the country unhindered is a cherished right. Persons who move out of the United States do so not only unnoticed but also unrecorded. In fact, statistics on emigration from the United States were last collected during the Eisenhower administration. Despite the deficiencies in the data, enough information is available to determine that during the 20th century the United States gained about 30 million immigrants and lost approximately 10 million people to emigration. Currently, more than 150,000 people, mostly former immigrants, leave each year. (1985, p. 2)

Number in thousands

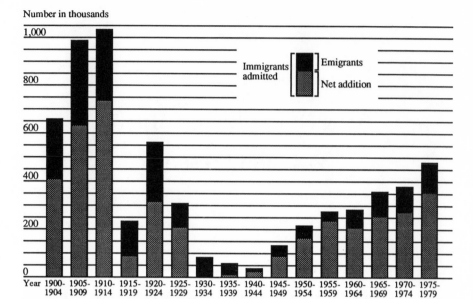

Figure 2.1. Annual average number of U.S. immigrants admitted, U.S. emigrants departing, and net addition to U.S. population, for five-year periods, 1900–1979. SOURCE: U.S. Immigration and Naturalization Service and U.S. Bureau of Census data as presented by Warren and Kraly (1985, p. 4).

RELATIONSHIP BETWEEN IMMIGRATION AND EMIGRATION

Despite the irregularities of the ebb and flow of migration from and to American shores, researchers have been able to chart this movement. Immigration to the United States reached its peak in 1907 with 1.3 million migrants. The same year Congress mandated the collection of data on emigrating non-U.S. citizens to better determine net migration figures (Warren and Kraly, 1985, p. 3). The shifts in the relationship between United States immigration and emigration during the twentieth century by five-year periods is presented in Figure 2.1. The data indicate that the former far exceeded the latter throughout the early period of the twentieth century. During the period overlapping World War I (1918 and 1919), emigration exceeded immigration. After World War I, immigration and emigration resumed although they never reached the prewar levels. By the end of the 1920s legislative restrictions had reduced immigration and by the 1930s emigration again exceeded immigration. After World War II, immigration slowly increased to accommodate various refugee populations although it remained substantially lower than the early twentieth century peaks.

Table 2.1. Estimates of U.S. Immigration, U.S. Emigration, and Net Additions to the U.S. Population, 1900–1979

Period	Net addition[a]	Immigrants	Emigration Total	Emigration Non-U.S. citizen	Emigration U.S. citizen
All periods	20,169	30,450	10,281	9,492	789
1975–1979	1,782	2,411	629	629	*
1970–1974	1,376	1,923	547	547	*
1965–1969	1,285	1,795	510	510	*
1960–1964	1,028	1,418	390	390	*
1955–1959	1,190	1,401	211	211	*
1950–1954	885	1,099	214	214	*
1945–1949	468	653	185	94	91
1940–1944	109	205	96	57	39
1935–1939	66	272	206	153	53
1930–1934	−16	427	443	336	107
1925–1929	1,009	1,520	511	390	121
1920–1924	1,601	2,775	1,174	893	281
1915–1919	458	1,173	715	618	97
1910–1914	3,733	5,175	1,442	1,442	*
1905–1909	3,154	4,947	1,793	1,793	*
1900–1904	2,041	3,256	1,215	1,215	*

*Not available.

[a]Numbers in thousands.

SOURCE: U.S. Immigration and Naturalization Service and U.S. Bureau of Census data as presented by Warren and Kraly (1985, p. 5).

Table 2.1 presents the estimates of immigration and emigration for the United States, including net migration for the same period 1900–1979 as described in Figure 2.1. It includes estimates, however, on the emigration of U.S. citizens. Data were collected by the U.S. Immigration and Naturalization Service between 1918 and 1950 but not since then. The data in Table 2.1, therefore, according to Warren and Kraly (1985) underestimate emigration in the more recent period because of the absence of hard figures. While emigration of non-U.S. citizens has been an important element in demographic change, emigration of U.S. citizens seems also to have been growing.

Table 2.2 presents the average annual emigration to selected countries from the United States for the period 1960–1976. The data for 18 of the 19 countries, for which data are presented, are drawn from records of the UN Statistical Office during that period. Figures for the nineteenth country, Israel, are derived from data made available to the authors by the Central Bureau of Statistics in Israel. The tabulations reveal that the seven leading countries of destination for Ameri-

Table 2.2. Average Annual Immigration to Selected Countries
from the United States, 1960–1976

Country of destination	Total years reported	Average annual immigration from the United States[a]			
		1960 to 1976	1970 to 1974	1965 to 1969	1960 to 1964
All countries		180,200	281,000	151,700	66,100
Argentina	14	400	600	300	300
Australia	15	8,500	12,800	8,500	4,400
Belgium	16	3,100	4,300	3,200	1,700
Brazil	13	1,000	900	1,100	1,100
Canada	11	21,900	24,600	19,900	*
France	14	900	1,400	900	400
Germany	15	24,800	27,800	26,400	21,600
Hong Kong	12	2,900	3,400	2,000	*
Israel	17	3,898	5,449	4,550	2,154
Italy	17	2,700	5,400	1,400	300
Japan	17	1,720	23,400	15,100	12,100
Kenya	17	500	400	800	200
Mexico	13	64,600	142,000	40,600	17,300
Netherlands	13	3,400	3,800	3,100	*
New Zealand	15	1,400	2,300	1,300	1,000
Nigeria	13	1,400	1,700	1,100	1,300
Norway	17	2,900	3,200	2,800	2,600
Sweden	17	1,700	1,700	1,600	1,800
United Kingdom	12	20,900	21,300	21,500	*

*Data are available for fewer than three years of the five-year period.

[a] Averages are based on the number of years for which data are reported.

SOURCE: Data derived from *United Nations Demographic Yearbook* as presented by Warren and Kraly (1985, p. 11) except for Israeli data, which were provided by the Israel Central Bureau of Statistics.

can emigrants between 1960 and 1976 were, in descending order: Mexico, Germany, United Kingdom, Canada, Japan, Australia, and Israel. They have absorbed 88% of the average annual output of American emigrants during the period discussed. Nearly one half of the emigrants went to the nearby countries of Mexico and Canada; about one quarter went to such European destinations as Germany and the United Kingdom; and most of the rest of the emigrants for the countries reported went to Japan, Australia, and Israel.

EMIGRATION: A PARALLEL TO SUICIDE?

In his classic work, *Suicide*, Emile Durkheim (1951) analyzed the social forces and facts that determine why some people choose to kill themselves. After reading Durkheim, one is struck by the observation that perhaps some of the factors that determine who voluntarily depart this life may be similar to those affecting people who voluntarily depart their country. Read this passage from Durkheim with the appropriate substitutions inserted in parentheses:

> The conclusion from all these facts is that the (emigration) . . . rate can be explained only sociologically. At any given moment the moral constitution of society establishes the contingent of voluntary (departures). (1951, p. 299)

Of course, we are not trying to suggest that emigration is the equivalent of "social suicide." It may seem at first glance inappropriate in such a study as ours that seeks to provide a more social psychological explanation of emigration to quote Durkheim, but Gerstein (1983) has argued that *Suicide* is not simply a sociological monograph:

> The significance of its contribution has much less to do with explaining observed rates of suicide than with defining the basic elements of a viable, truly social psychological framework of analysis. . . .

> This claim about Durkheim's *Suicide* implies, indeed, requires that Durkheim held a basic theory about the nature of the individual, a basic theory of social organization, and a vision of the dynamic linkages that manage the problematic stability of human societies. (1983, p. 241)

Durkheim argued that the suicide rate varied with the degree of integration in society. Likewise, voluntary emigration may be seen in the same light. People become detached from meaningful social groups, and this encourages a few to make the choice to move abroad. Rates of suicide and emigration may both be indices of the degree of integration in society. It should not be assumed that desperation is the dominant motive for both patterned responses to "detachment." Despairing people who, in social psychological terms, are adrift sometimes do seek escape through emigration (as well as suicide, crime, and other forms of self-destructive behaviors). Sobel (1985), for example, emphasized this theme in his work on emigration from Israel. People who are truly estranged can satisfy their needs for personal identity and satisfying relationships in what to *them* are less alienating societies.

The weakly integrated individual may seek more positive goals than just to escape and get away from it all. He or she may value important relationships to spouses or decide to indulge in a bit of free-booting wanderlust abroad, fully intending to return to America to start a "real life." Disintegration may be a

Table 2.3. General Motivations for Migration

Locus of concern	Goals of migration	
	Expressive	Instrumental
Self	Individuals seeking greater political and/or religious expression Rootless wanderers A	"Brain drain" workers Foreign students Migrant laborers B
	C	D
Others	Spouses and children seeking family unity Disciples of charismatic leaders Adherents of religious and political groups	Peace Corps volunteers Missionaries

temporary condition that people perceive and act upon as an opportunity to pursue a dream. Anomie is not the only consequence of weak integration.

It is hypothesized that most migrating Americans are weakly bound by the social relationships that we usually attribute to people who are well integrated in society. In order to compare different migrant streams, it is useful to concentrate on the foci of their activity or the goals they pursue. Their goals often reflect high levels of commitment to some groups, for example, nuclear family, work, and religious affiliation, and low levels of involvement in the local community, family of origin, state, or nation in which they currently find themselves.

Table 2.3 conceptualizes these general motivations for migration as they might apply to a variety of migrating groups. With respect to the goals of migration, "expressive" refers to fulfillment of personal, emotional, and spiritual needs; in general, emigration is perceived to lead to value fulfillment. "Instrumental" goals refer to the importance of achieving an external objective usually resulting in material gain or task achievement. With respect to the locus of concern, "self" and "others" refer to whom the migrant essentially seeks to satisfy: oneself or another. This scheme distorts the reality of migration activities, for emigration (here, meaning simply moving abroad, not necessarily for good) typically involves complex motives, feelings, and goals. But this analytical ideal type permits comparisons of disparate activities, groups, and destinations. It is suggested that this typology can be extended to all migration patterns.

Consider how different groups that have arrived in (or left) America might be aligned in this typology.

For example in quadrant A, "self-expressive" motives may include those individuals seeking greater political and/or religious expression for their beliefs or those without any strong social ties that root them to a particular society. Quadrant B, "self-instrumental," includes those individuals whose external objectives may revolve about work or study, such as the "brain drain" phenomenon, foreign study, or migrant laborers. Quadrant C, "others-expressive," refers to those individuals whose expressive needs center around others more than themselves as in the case of those spouses and children who emigrate to preserve family unity, fully committed adherents of religious and political groups, or disciples of charismatic leaders. Quadrant D, "others-instrumental," includes those individuals whose external objectives revolve more about serving others than themselves as in the case of Peace Corps volunteers or missionaries serving a particular religious and/or medical causes.

This conceptual model of the general motivations for migration seeks to go beyond the push-pull model which simply asks whether people are more pushed from their country of origin or pulled toward their new destination. This explanation derives from a gestalt or configurationist social psychological approach that tries to analyze behavior according to the balance of social forces operating on people akin to physics. Our current approach derives from the symbolic interactionist type of social psychology, which is rooted in sociology. As such, it analyzes human behavior in terms of the meanings shared by people and the identities they seek to validate. Indeed, the bulk of our findings reported in the subsequent chapters will revolve around an exposition of these meanings and identities.

While Table 2.3 tries to capture the full gamut of the motivations for migration, it should be kept in mind that our study concerns itself with voluntaristic international migrants. This book concentrates on Americans who have gone abroad with the intention to work or remain in the receiving country for more than one year, and who have sometimes remained there permanently. It is of particular interest that these people make free choices to move to other industrialized (but less affluent) societies. They are not refugees; they are neither impoverished, nor persecuted. Their motives for going are less obvious because they lack the desperate pushes of so many who have historically migrated to the United States.

OVERVIEW OF DATA AND METHODS

The issues addressed in this study should, under the most optimal conditions, be studied through a common set of questions to be administered to probability samples in the selected countries. Unfortunately, the magnitude of such a project, both financially and administratively, far exceeds the resources at the disposal of this team of researchers. Therefore, the next best option was undertaken, that is, to analyze comparable data sets available to us for at least two countries with similar patterns of substantial voluntary international migration, Australia and Israel, which are considerably different from the United States. Both of these countries are similar in that they have the largest immigrant presence of the advanced industrialized societies (Evans, 1984). (Where data are available, additional references are made to the Canadian situation.) Each instance of American emigration was initially examined separately, but the emphasis in this study is on their commonalities and meaningful differences.

A variety of methods and sources including demographic and survey research provide the data bases for answering the questions posed in this book. In the case of American emigration to Australia, the data sources include:

1. *Australian Survey*: The survey sample ($N = 328$) was randomly selected from all Americans, 18 years and older (in 1975), who possessed Settler Visas, that is, they were considered to be settlers by the Australian government and by other researchers as well.[1]
2. *Interview Study*: Between September 1974 and December 1975, 50 Americans were interviewed, all but one of whom lived in and around Melbourne. These interviews were loosely structured, but guided, and concentrated on how Americans decide to go to Australia and how they decide to stay or return to America.[2]
3. *Australian Immigration Consolidated Statistics*: Published by the Department of Immigration and Ethnic Affairs, this annual volume summarizes such immigration statistics as birthplace of the Australian population, immigration programs and actual arrivals, marital status and sex of immigrants, family composition of assisted settler arrivals, and so on.
4. *Other Sources*: Several other studies have focused on American migration to Australia. These include surveys conducted by the Australian Department of Labour and Immigration (1969, 1971, and 1973), Bardo and Bardo (1980 a–e, 1981), Cuddy (1977), and Finifter and Finifter (1980 a,b, 1982).

---

[1]Most cases ($N = 1,037$) were drawn from the compiled Passenger Arrival Cards. The rest ($N = 69$) were taken from a list of naturalized citizens. Of the final sample of 1,100 names, 332 were returned as nondeliverable (invalid addresses, returned to the United States) and 440 did not respond. If the nondeliverables are deleted, the response rate is 43%. Comparisons with published statistics of Americans living in Australia (Australian Department of Labour and Immigration, 1973) suggest that this was a reasonably representative sample.

[2]Respondents were drawn through "snowball" or chain referral sampling, whose techniques and problems are described by Biernacki and Waldorf (1981).

In the case of American emigration to Israel, the data sources include:

1. *Israel Immigrant Absorption Survey*: This has been a standard survey periodically carried out by the Israel Central Bureau of Statistics. A sample of immigrants is selected and formed into a panel that is followed for three years and periodically reinterviewed. Data were obtained from the Israel Central Bureau of Statistics covering those American immigrants who were part of the panels that began in the years 1969, 1970, and 1971. The initial sample selections for the three different panels yielded the sample respondents from the United States ($N = 560$).
2. *Americans in Israel Study*: This project relied on in-depth interviews with a total of 131 respondents including persons preparing for migration to Israel ($N = 36$), living in Israel ($N = 49$), and having returned from Israel ($N = 46$), all in the period 1974–1977. Also, use has been made of Israeli governmental statistics on immigrants by country of origin and by year of arrival (see footnote 2).
3. *PNAI Study*: Questionnaires gathered at the 1984 convention in Israel of the Association of Parents of North American Israelis ($N = 107$).[3]

Whenever additional data on emigration from the United States to other destinations in the developed world were made available to us, they were included in our discussion. For example, we included in this chapter data on American emigration to Canada, based on the annual reports of Immigration Statistics (1969–1984), that provide information on all landed immigrants in Canada. (A discussion of the extent of comparability of the Canadian case follows later in the chapter.)

All of these data sources were then analyzed applying a variety of techniques, which are described subsequently.[4] Appropriate comparisons are developed throughout. The utilization of a variety of research methods has come to be known in the social science literature as "triangulation." Literally it refers to a technique utilized in surveying and navigation in which different measurements are taken of the same object by constructing triangles in which one line is of known length and the others are not. Any particular research method and system

---

[3]For further details, see Tabory (1988/1989).

[4]It may be asked whether data largely gathered in the 1970s has any relevance for the 1990s. Since we are seeking to analyze the relationships among variables, the recency of the data is not so important. In other words, we would expect the emigrants to Australia or Israel to be younger than the American population as a whole whether we drew a sample in 1970, 1980, or 1990. Nevertheless, we do, however, provide more recent data on the extent of such emigration from the United States in this chapter. Furthermore, we believe based on our own ongoing observations of these migration streams that replication of our research today would be largely consistent with our earlier work.

of study is apt to provide a skewed and, hence, incomplete or limited picture of what is really going on. In terms of social science research methods, a partial picture lacks scientific validity. Studying the same phenomenon by different methods reduces the risk that a particular method affected the results of the study or led the data to be viewed in a particular way. Thus, a variety of methods provides one with different perspectives by which to come to a more coherent explanation of the phenomenon under study. Similar results produced by all the methods, no matter how one studies the phenomenon, increases the probability that one has a scientifically valid result. This is one of the major benefits obtained by drawing on our various data sources.

The research procedures of this study involve several methods and techniques: survey research including in-depth interviewing, secondary analysis, and participant observation. As Babbie (1986) notes, each research method in the social sciences has its own particular strength and weakness. The process of using several different research methods, or triangulation as noted above, is designed to overcome or at least reduce the danger of the research finding reflecting any one, specific method of inquiry. While we are studying the same phenomenon, emigration, we are not actually measuring the *same individuals* in different ways. Thus, the Australian data permit a more qualitative approach to the problem while the Israeli data permit a more quantitative approach.

The use of different methods also enables us to relate to the two major models of explanation in the social sciences. The *ideographic* model aims at explanation through the enumeration of all the various considerations that relate to a specific action, including unique factors that are limited to a given occurrence. The *nomothetic* model, on the other hand, involves the isolation of the relatively few considerations that provide a partial explanation for the behavior of many people. As Babbie (1986, p. 54) explains, the goal of the nomothetic model is to provide the greatest amount of explanation using the fewest number of causal variables to uncover general patterns of cause and effect.

It is clear that statistical analysis in itself relates to the nomothetic model. By using statistical data, and especially through multivariate analysis, we seek to identify the major factors that affect most people in the migration process. The migration process, however, is very complex, and we would be remiss if we did not utilize ideographic methods as well to provide a thorough picture of all the factors at work in deciding to move, encountering the absorption process, and wrestling with the question of whether to remain or return. This means that at times we are unable to indicate how much of the variance of the decision process is attributable to a particular variable. This is offset by our provision of a more nearly complete picture of the migration process and the multitude of social psychological factors that impinge on the individual emigrant as he or she struggles with this stressful experience.

AMERICAN EMIGRATION TO AUSTRALIA

Americans find it easy to understand why people immigrate to the United States. Immigrants are part of America's national myth, and a substantial basis of population growth. The popular conception is that everybody comes from somewhere. Americans perhaps suspect that most of the world's underprivileged would move here if they could; millions of illegal aliens from Mexico and other Latin countries seem to prove this hunch. Rich and powerful, enormously affluent, and exuberantly free, America seems to hold out the promise of unlimited freedom and material gain for anybody who works hard. So it is not a simple thing to explain why many Americans leave their homeland to settle in another country. Indeed, one of their more prominent destinations is Australia.

A 1971 Gallup Poll asked a sample of Americans: "If you were free to do so, would you like to go and settle in another country? Which country?" One out of eight answered "yes," and Australia was their most popular choice (followed by Canada, the United Kingdom, and Switzerland). This was not the first time Gallup had asked this question. Ada Finifter (1976) has summarized the results of the six earlier times this had been done. Between 1960 and 1971 the percentage answering "yes" doubled, from 6% to 12%. In fact, the number of Americans migrating to Australia had become substantial during the latter 1960s and early 1970s (see Table 2.4). One estimate is that the net American settler population of Australia grew from 10,810 in 1961 to 17,412 in 1966, and 27,009 by 1973. Finifter and Finifter (1980a) quote a figure of 50,000 by 1978. From an average of about 1,000 arriving American settlers in 1959, there was roughly a sixfold increase by 1971. The subsequent decades, however, have experienced a decline, and the number of emigrants now fluctuates between 1,000 and 2,000 per year.

Between 1947 and 1982, more than 3,000,000 people moved to Australia. The largest group, more than 1,000,000, were from England, Scotland, and Ireland. But immigrants have also come from non-Anglo European countries as well. In descending order of size (after the Anglo countries), they came from Italy, Yugoslavia, Greece, Germany, and the Netherlands. At 32,620, the American settler population in 1982 was fourteenth in size, slightly more numerous than Egyptians and Malaysians, and much fewer than Poles, Indians, or Maltese.

Suddenly Americans became a major migrating group to Australia, although still one of the smaller immigrant groups in that country of immigrants. By 1970, 20% of Australia's population was foreign-born, compared with 5% of America's 1970 population. Indeed, the Americans attracted the attention of the mass media, the public, and the Australian government, which suddenly found its American consulates flooded by requests for information about possible migration. Both interest in and migration to Australia peaked in 1971–1972, and

Table 2.4. American Migrants to
Australia, 1961–1985

Year	Total settlers
1961	1,033[a]
1962	1,033[a]
1963	1,109
1964	1,400
1965	1,805
1966	2,439
1967	2,472
1968	2,586
1969	3,190
1970	3,591
1971	5,447
1972	6,564
1973	3,828
1974	3,324
1975	3,192
1976	1,440
1977	1,180
1978	1,031
1979	1,079
1980	1,226
1981	1,607
1982	1,802
1983	1,920
1984	1,750
1985	1,540

[a] 1961–1962 data are estimated from a three-year panel (1959–1962); 1962–1982 data are based on fiscal years reported; 1983–1985 data are derived from the Australian Consulate in New York.
SOURCE: 1961–1983 Australian Government Statistics.

then began to fall off. But while the surge lasted, it was dramatic. Newspapers and popular magazines sometimes found that migrating Americans made good copy: "In Search of the New Frontier" (*Sydney Morning Herald*, 1 July, 1971); or "Americans are Emigrating to Australia: In Search of the U.S.A. More and More" (Harry Gordon, *The New York Times Sunday Magazine*, 17 May, 1970). These were troubled times in the United States, and this migrating movement supposedly reflected that turbulence, which helped to break some of the bonds that tied Americans to their country.

AMERICAN EMIGRATION TO ISRAEL

American emigration to Israel did not begin with the creation of the state of Israel in 1948. Indeed, it goes back at least more than a century before to the time of Turkish hegemony over Palestine. One of the earliest emigrants was the first American consul for the Middle East region. Originally a Protestant, he moved to Jerusalem in 1845, and within two years converted to Judaism and founded an agricultural community. Eventually about 50 Americans joined this pioneer colony (Lapide, 1961).

To be sure, this was atypical. Most American emigrants were Jews who wanted to live or die in the Holy Land, but little is known about them prior to World War I. Indeed, probably fewer than 50 Americans emigrated per year in this period. Nevertheless, during the period of the British mandate, from 1919–1948, the average number per year quadrupled, reaching about 220.

Even after the establishment of the state of Israel, emigration reached only about 425 per year in the period 1948–1960.[5] It was not the creation of the state, or even the 1967 Six-Day War, that heralded a new pattern of such emigration. During the period of 1961–1967, the average annual number of emigrants was 3,000, an increase of more than sevenfold (see Table 2.5). This was likely due to the effects of the growng sense of idealism, the expansion of academic and work-study programs in Israel, and the emergence of a generation of graduates of Jewish day schools and other intensive Jewish educational programs from the large pool of baby-boom children born after World War II. Indeed, after the Six-Day War, from 1968 to 1971, the number more than doubled again, to about 6,300 per year. Of course, since 1974 with the volatility of the global economic situation, the demographic decrease in younger adults, and Israel's recent economic and political difficulties, emigration has declined.

Beginning with the first day of independence of the state of Israel (May 15, 1948) through 1972, nearly 1.5 million immigrants arrived, more than tripling the Jewish population of Israel (Bachi, 1974, p. 5). During this period the United States was the seventh leading exporter of migrants to Israel after Morocco, Poland, Russia, Iran, Turkey, and Bulgaria (Zinger, 1974, p. 64), but the Americas were far outpaced by the other continents (Europe, Africa, and Asia in descending order) in providing migrants. Europe sent over 600,000 migrants, and the Afro-Asian migration accounted for over 700,000.

Table 2.5 highlights the recent trends in emigration of Americans to Israel. The peak was reached in 1971 with over 7,000 emigrants paralleling the increase to other countries, such as Mexico, Canada, Australia, and nearly every country

---

[5]For a study of Americans in Israel during the 1948–1949 Israeli War of Independence, see Heckelman (1974).

Table 2.5. North American Migrants
to Israel, 1961–1985[a]

Year	Number
1961	1,871
1962	2,352
1963	2,850
1964	3,282
1965	3,522
1966	3,227
1967	4,048
1968	6,216
1969	5,739
1970	6,424
1971	7,364
1972	5,515
1973	4,393
1974	3,089
1975	2,802
1976	2,700
1977	2,571
1978	2,921
1979	2,950
1980	2,312
1981	2,384
1982	2,693
1983	3,469
1984	2,581
1985	2,175

[a]Migrants include immigrants and temporary residents defined officially after 1969 as "potential immigrants." In some years a small number of Canadians are included.
SOURCES: *Israel Central Bureau of Statistics,* 1967–1985. *Israel Central Bureau of Statistics,* 1961–1966, cited in Goldscheider (1974, pp. 337–384).

reported in Table 2.2. In the past decade emigration has fluctuated between approximately 2,300–3,500 per year. The 1983 Israeli Census reported 37,327 U.S.-born persons living permanently in Israel.[6]

[6]For a fairly comprehensive bibliography on American migrants to Israel, see Kaufmann (1987).

AMERICAN EMIGRATION TO CANADA

While American emigration to Canada may be regarded as a concomitant of the Vietnam War, it has a history reaching back to the earliest period of American independence from Great Britain. According to Christy, "During the American Revolution another migration did occur: the United Empire Loyalists, estimated at around 100,000, chose to leave for Canada rather than become citizens of the rebellious colonies" (1972, p. 16).

In the nineteenth century a smaller number of Americans migrated to Canada to escape the oppression of slavery through the use of the "underground railroads." Canada became an important terminus after Congress passed a strict fugitive slave law in the Compromise of 1850.

Of course, in the twentieth century the period of the late 1960s and early 1970s marked the apex of emigration to Canada. Table 2.6 reviews these recent data and reveals that such emigration peaked between 1970 and 1974, when the figure reached 26,541.

Figure 2.2 permits a comparison of the incidence of American emigration for selected available years for Australia, Canada, and Israel. In general, the level of emigration to Canada was four to eight times greater than to Australia or Israel during the peak of emigration to these countries (1969–1973). By contrast, the difference has declined greatly for the most recent period (1983–1984) with emigration to Canada only two to four times as great as to Israel and Australia. In the past decade emigration to Canada has fluctuated between 6,000–10,000 Americans per year.

Migration across the U.S.-Canadian border has been going on for more than 200 years. Suffice it to say that the frequent contact for over two centuries and the increased economic and cultural integration of Canada and the United States make traversing their common border much less meaningful than migrating to Australia or Israel. Indeed, this political border does not generally represent a sociologically significant boundary as far as international migration goes. The American migrants experience little or no culture shock compared to what is produced by the migration to Australia or Israel. Nevertheless, the Canadian data on emigration provide a backdrop against which to view the pattern of emigration in a case where physical distance and cultural difference are both minimal. Ultimately, however, we chose not to pursue this case in our analysis because the mainstream of this movement is more akin to internal rather than international migration.

The reason for this is that migration involves more than physical movement. It also entails a state of mind. Migrants to Israel, Australia, and even Mexico know that they are going to a "foreign" country. Even when they think they know the language (ask a British citizen whether Americans really know English!),

Table 2.6. American Migrants to
Canada, 1961–1985

Year	Number of American migrants
1961	11,516
1962	11,643
1963	11,736
1964	12,565
1965	15,143
1966	17,514
1967	19,038
1968	20,422
1969	22,785
1970	24,424
1971	24,336
1972	22,618
1973	25,242
1974	26,541
1975	20,155
1976	17,315
1977	12,888
1978	9,945
1979	9,617
1980	9,926
1981	10,559
1982	9,360
1983	7,381
1984	6,922
1985	6,664

SOURCE: Immigration Statistics Canada, 1961–1985.

they know that they will encounter a culture that is different and that requires adjustment. This is much less the case with regard to migration to Canada. The (increasingly) overlapping cultural orientation of both countries may well lead migrants to feel that they have to make about as much change as when they move from Chicago to Los Angeles. The telephone system is basically the same and Canadian numbers are reached by dialing a simple area code (it is not considered an international call); it is domestic airlines that connect the two countries; and the ball teams are integrated in the American professional leagues. Television viewers along the border can only be sure about which country they are watching when there is a station identification break. Try shopping on both sides of the border without looking too closely at the writing on the wrappers and figure out where you are. This is not to say that migrants to Canada do not encounter

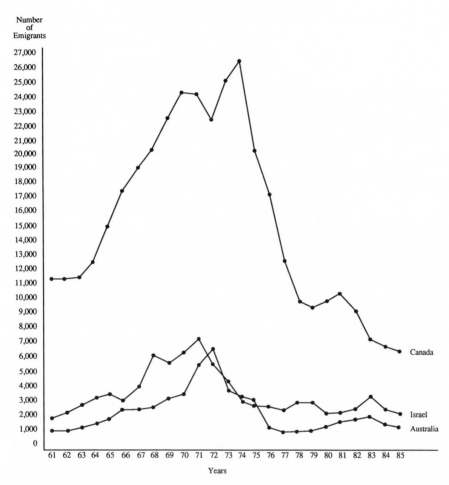

Figure 2.2. American emigration to Canada, Israel, and Australia, 1961–1985.

difficulties. However, it is our belief that the motivation for migration is funda-mentally different when deciding to move to such countries as Australia and Israel, in contrast to Canada, and it is for that reason that we concentrate on the former. Furthermore, the lack of comparable data precludes the possibility of additional analysis of the Canadian case.[7]

[7]We are interested in the overseas migrations of all Americans who have been brought up within the framework of American society and its culture. We would recommend research on American migrants to Mexico, England, France, Italy, and so forth. There are English-speaking enclaves in a number of countries as exemplified by their having English-language newspapers. Unfortunately, to

It is tempting to attribute the peak years of emigration to these countries in the late 1960s and early 1970s to a variety of political and social upheavals occurring in American society, evoking an image of Durkheim's anomic social processes driving many to the limits of endurance. But a close analysis of migrants' initial goals, adjustments, and evolving commitments minimizes these anomic "pushes." Instead, as we look at how these Americans explained their behavior, we find a complex array of circumstances, motives, and unanticipated outcomes.[8]

SUMMARY

While the Statue of Liberty is a symbol of the United States as a land of immigration, it is likely to have been a silent witness to as many as 100 departures for every 300 arrivals. Being mute, it could not call attention to the extent of emigration (10 million people) at the same time that there was substantial immigration (30 million) to the United States during the course of the twentieth century. Indeed, right after World War I and during the 1930s, *emigration exceeded immigration*. During the period 1960–1976, seven countries absorbed nearly nine tenths of American emigrants: Mexico, Germany, United Kingdom, Canada, Japan, Australia, and Israel, in descending order. Availability and comparability of data only permit us to study the latter two cases.

Durkheim's insight that individual behavior is related to the strength of the social bond is significant for explaining American emigration. However, weakly integrated individuals are not necessarily alienated; and alienation is not a satisfactory explanation for why Americans move abroad, why they remain there, or why they return. Instead, it should be seen as just one of several processes involved in these migration patterns. So we suggest a typology of goals, or foci, of migrants' activities: self-expressive, others-expressive, self-instrumental, and others-instrumental. This typology permits a clearer comparison of different groups of Americans, for the type of voluntary permanent international migration between developed societies, which is the subject of this book. Emigrants from

---

the best of our knowledge, American migrants have only been studied in Australia, Israel, and Canada. The two countries we present here do represent widely differing societies and our data permit us to study our research questions in depth.

[8]As the research to be introduced in the coming pages indicates, a variety of triggering situations can lead to a decision to emigrate. We are more concerned about the circumstances that lead our migrants to choose the "new countries" they did. Of course, severe personal problems could have existed for a few of our migrants. The authorities in charge of examining migrant applicants screen for individuals with mental health problems. The people we are dealing with do not enter either Australia or Israel as mere tourists. The research introduced in this book was conducted with proper professional standards, and we judge our data to be both reliable and valid.

the United States are characterized by all four of these goals although some goals appear to predominate in contributing to migration to some countries. The data cited above indicate that there are sufficient cases to be studied.

The main focus of this book is the comparative analysis of emigration to Australia and Israel from the United States, examining factors in motivation, absorption and adjustment, and return migration. While American emigration to Israel has been known since the mid-nineteenth century, it only became a phenomenon of visible proportions during the period of the 1960s and thereafter. Likewise, emigration to Australia escalated during this same period. During a similar six-year period between mid-1967 and 1973, the average annual number of American settlers in Australia was 4,201. During approximately the same period the average annual number of American emigrants to Israel was somewhat greater at 5,913. During a similar period, for which data are available, emigration to Canada averaged about four to five times as great at 19,906.

In order to undertake this study, a variety of data sources was utilized: Australian Sample Survey ($N = 328$), Australian Interview Study ($N = 50$), Israel Immigrant Absorption Survey ($N = 560$), Americans in Israel Study ($N = 121$), and the PNAI (Parents of North American Israeli migrants) Study ($N = 107$). These data were collected during the period 1969–1984.

The questions raised in Chapter 1 remain:

1. What accounts for the motivations of migrants to move?
2. What are the sources of the adjustment problems the migrants experience?
3. What explains whether the migrants remain or return?

3

Motives

Why They Move

> Australia seemed like a good place to come. I knew it was time to do something. Life was good and I knew if I didn't do something I would probably never do anything. I just thought it would be a nice thing to do. I can't go any deeper than that because that's as deep as it went.

These are the observations of a 31-year-old single female travel agent who had been living in Australia for six years. Her explanation represents a typical response of the American emigrants in Australia whom we called "Yanks" in our study.

And these are the observations of a middle-aged businessman, who gave up a seven-room house and three cars.

> In Israel in everything that I do from walking in the street to visiting the Wall, I have a feeling of belonging; and it is easier to raise my children here. I came here because of a growing disaffection with the Jewish community and the greater American community and an increasing identification (from Jewish literature) with Israel allowed me to see Israel as an option.

Here we see the striking contrast in motivation that generally distinguishes Americans who emigrate to Australia from Americans emigrating to Israel. The former include a greater proportion of people propelled by a search for something new or for a challenge to overcome. The latter are ruled by the perceived religioethnic opportunities of living in Israel that are unmet in the United States. The American immigrants to Israel we studied are called *Olim* (*Oleh* if masculine singular and *Olah* if feminine singular), literally those who go up (as in biblical days when Jews went on a pilgrimage and ascended the Judean mountains to Jerusalem to bring a sacrifice); the act of ascent or immigration specifically to Israel is called *aliya*. (The Hebrew term for migration in general is *hagira*, but emigration *from* Israel is termed *yerida*, or descent, and emigrants are *yordim*, or descenders.)

The motives of the Yanks and Olim are diverse, but in some ways these two groups have much in common. Uncovering the similarities and differences in these cross-national comparisons is the object of our study. Indeed, this objective is consistent with that laid out by Kohn (1987) in his presidential address to the American Sociological Association. As Kohn notes, similarities suggest regularities that transcend differences in history, culture, and experience, while differences require that history be placed in the forefront of any explanation (pp. 728–729).

Two classes of migration are of particular interest in the understanding of migration to Australia and Israel: *impelled migration* and *free migration*. Impelled migration refers to the case in which adverse conditions for a subject prevail in the country of origin, yet the migrant retains the power to decide whether or not to leave (Petersen, 1970, p. 58). Free migration takes place when it is only the will of the migrant that is the decisive factor to move (Petersen, 1970, p. 62).

Utilizing a social psychological perspective, we would argue that free migration is never completely free. People do not pick up and move without any reason. Rather, there is some subjective reason that impels the migrant. Migration may be for a short period, without even intentionally intending to move away forever. We shall encounter Australians in this regard whom we will designate as sojourners. They differ from tourists, whose travels initiate with the clear intention of returning after a fixed period of time, or who intend to utilize their time to see the world. Tourists generally do not intend to work or set up a structured semipermanent home as do migrants. The migrants, including the sojourners, feel some need to get away. This "need" may not be easily discernible to an outsider observer. Thus, social situations in which the migrants find themselves combine with their individual personalities and lead them to decide, individually, that they must move.

MIGRATION SELECTIVITY: BACKGROUND CHARACTERISTICS[1]

Most Americans who emigrate to Australia (with Settler Visas) are relatively young, well-educated, and highly trained. The same can be said for Americans who go to Israel. Table 3.1 compares the two groups of emigrants on five life-cycle and socioeconomic variables for which data were available.

Both groups were young adults. The Australian group was younger with 57% of survey respondents under 30. For the Israeli group the corresponding figure was 42%. The percentage of U.S. adults in the 18–29 age category was only 30%. This means that these emigrants were one and one-half to two times as likely to be young, independent adults.

[1]This section is adapted from Dashefsky, DeAmicis, and Lazerwitz (1984).

Table 3.1. Contrasting American Emigrants in Australia and Israel (in Percent)[a]

Characteristics	Americans in Israel[b]	Americans in Australia[c]	Adult Americans in U.S.[d]
18–29 years	42	57	30
Male	45	60	48
Married	60	60	66
College degree	42	36	17
Professional job in U.S.	40	40	16

[a]This table originally appeared in Dashefsky *et al.* (1984) and is reprinted with permission.
[b]Immigrant Absorption Survey of Israel Central Bureau of Statistics.
[c]Australian Sample Survey.
[d]Derived from Statistical Abstract of the United States, 1982–1983.

People in both groups were about equally likely to be married: 57% of Americans in Australia and 60% in Israel were married at the time of arrival. The corresponding proportion for all Americans was 66%. These emigrants were slightly more likely to be single, but still, typically, they went as small family units. The two groups were about the same age and had also had similar educational background and professional training: 36% of the Australian group and 42% of the Israeli group had a bachelor's degree. This is well above the American figure of 17%.[2] In occupational background, identical percentages, 40%, in the two groups reported holding a professional job in the United States. This is well above the proportion for all Americans, 16%. Thus, the emigrants were considerably more likely to have held a professional job (in the United States) than other Americans even though they were younger than American adults as a whole.

Only one area for which data were available revealed a distinct difference between the two migrating groups and that was sex. Men comprised 60% of the surveyed Americans in Australia, but only 45% of Americans surveyed living in Israel. These proportions depart from the 48/52 male/female split among adult Americans. In many historical instances of international migration, males have predominated. Nevertheless, Israel represents an ideologically acceptable destination for the emancipation of females from traditional Jewish households which other venues may not. The likelihood of some military service requirement for male immigrants (though usually not as demanding as that for native-born Israelis) may reduce American male migration to Israel. It is interesting to note that despite the prevailing notion that men predominate in international migration, Houstoun *et al.* (1984) reported that since 1930 more females have migrated to the United States than males.

Thus, it may be seen that in most respects the emigrants to Australia and Israel were similar on a variety of biosocial characteristics examined: age, mari-

[2]Also, 28% of our panel study group of Olim, had studied for, but did not complete, a college degree. That would raise the "college" percentage to 70% for the Olim, which is quite high. The Yanks reported 16% studying for but not completing a college degree for a "college" total of 52%.

tal status, level of formal education, and employment. They were, however, divergent from the adult American population in that they were much younger, slightly less likely to be married, more highly educated, and more likely to be professionally employed.

Religion was not a significant factor in the Yanks' decisions to move to Australia, according to our research and that of others. Finifter and Finifter (1980a, p. 5) note that "American migrants in Australia are considerably less likely than the U.S. population to have a preference for any organized religion." They found that 30% of their respondents claimed "no religious preference" and only 5% of their respondents cited "religious calling" as a "reason for migrating," making this the third least likely motive out of the 13 provided. By contrast, 28% of Americans in Israel claimed to be Orthodox (compared to 11% in 1971 of all American Jewish adults). Since this time, the Orthodox percentage is thought to have increased.

The American characteristics of both migrating groups show up in their reactions to the work ethics of Australia and Israel. Both the Yanks and Olim continually complained about the inefficiency and low work productivity in their adopted lands. These two migrating groups, despite their religious and ethnic differences, had fully absorbed the hardworking and efficiency-oriented attitudes of the United States. Indeed, they found themselves upset by the lack of these characteristics in the countries to which they migrated.

The migrating women disliked the lower status, relative to the United States, of women in their new societies. Indeed, in Israel, women migrants from the United States were instrumental in renewing the women's movement in that country.

Both groups were viewed as Americans by the native-born population of their new countries. Being an American meant membership in a high-status, well-liked group. The combination of these factors, and the background and educational characteristics of these two groups, enabled them to move rather rapidly into the solidly middle-class sectors of their new societies. They were able to avoid, for the most part, the more common working-class status that is the lot of the typical migrant.

Being professionally trained and college educated, these young adults were already potentially very mobile. Socialized in a culture that values travel, independence, and self-fulfillment, they were part of the American mainstream that had not yet set down their roots. Going abroad is not so hard to understand. Why they stayed there is perhaps the more challenging question.

MOTIVATION AND MIGRATION IN FOUR QUADRANTS

To understand why Americans migrated to Australia or Israel, it is necessary to clarify the concept of migration itself. The accepted understanding is that international migration is permanent relocation from one country to another for more than one year. It is generally assumed that migrants intend from the start to settle more or less permanently.

The Australian government uses the term "migrant" to mean anyone with a Permanent Resident Visa, issued to those who state their intention to remain in the country. The government treats this visa as evidence of a resolve to stay permanently, and this is the basis of their official migration statistics. This visa, however, has more than symbolic and head-counting value. It gives the holder the right to find employment in Australia in any job that does not require Australian citizenship. Moreover, it does not have to be renewed, unlike the Temporary Residence Visa, which in 1975 needed to be renewed every year. Americans who arrive with the Permanent Resident Visa can be found teaching in Australian high schools and universities, starring in Australian television shows, ministering in their churches, reporting for their newspapers, and plastering their swimming pools. Holders of this visa are eligible for passage assistance, as it is called. Depending on their country of origin, the Australian government subsidizes part or all of the expenses of migrating, finds them temporary lodging in one of the migrant hostels at very low cost, and makes them eligible for assistance under several migrant-assistance programs. The applicant is carefully screened: medical and police records, proof of educational status, full occupational background, and so forth. It is understandable that journalists, policymakers, demographers, and the public have all considered these migrants as people who intended to stay. All of the Yanks interviewed in Australia held Permanent Resident Visas.[3]

This definition of a migrant as a permanent settler is relevant for the study of demographic patterns, but not for social psychological analysis, since it assumes an intention that may not be valid. Therefore, it is useful to divide the emigrant population into categories based on their intentions or goals. Two analytically distinct groups were readily evident in the case of Yanks in Australia: settlers and sojourners. According to the Australian survey sample ($n = 328$), 35% of the respondents definitely intended to settle in Australia at the time of arrival. They are referred to as settlers. The remainder were undecided or definitely planned to return to the United States. These were the sojourners, who expected to leave Australia to continue with the rest of their lives. The split among the migrants to

---

[3]One policy-linked reason for this is the need to screen applicants for genuine migration from the much larger group of transient visitors and tourists. In order for aliens to work in Australia, they must qualify for a Temporary Resident Visa, valid for one year but renewable; or a Permanent Resident Visa, good for five years, and renewable indefinitely. Both require identical background investigations, demanding much time and documentation. A Tourist Visa is much easier to secure, but it is temporary, about six months, and does not allow employment in Australia. Government officials probably assume that anyone who would go through the inconvenience of acquiring a Permanent Resident Visa instead of a Tourist Visa must intend to stay. Therefore, anyone with a Permanent Resident Visa was assumed to be a genuine settler. All interviews with Americans were restricted to those who had Permanent Resident Visas. We operationalized the concept migrant to mean any American living in Australia under either type of settler visa.

Israel is very similar. Shortly after their arrival, 36% definitely felt they would stay in Israel.

A framework for analyzing motivations was initially suggested by reviewing the factors articulated by emigrants returning to the United States from Israel. The factors that they themselves felt accounted for their return to the States were initially categorized in descending order of intensity as "familial," "instrumental," "expressive," and "personal" (see Dashefsky and Lazerwitz, 1983). Further examination of these responses suggested that they really represented antinomies that could be applied to motivations for migration and challenges to adjustment as well as issues in return migration.

Table 3.2 summarizes the diversity of motivations that specifically may energize American emigrants, in terms of four quadrants presented in Chapter 2. In quadrant A, the migrant's focus is self-expressive, for example, fulfillment of one's religious identity, the satisfaction of travel, escape from a sense of demoralization, and so on. In quadrant B, the migrant's focus is self-instrumental, as in achieving a personal external goal such as starting a business or exploiting a job opportunity. In quadrant C, the focus is on others-expressive activities, such as marrying an Australian and subsequently moving to Australia to maintain family unity. In quadrant D, the others-instrumental focus includes those moving abroad primarily to serve as medical or educational service personnel. This

Table 3.2. Motivations for American Migration

Locus of concern	Goals of migration	
	Expressive	Instrumental
Self	Adventure/travel Alienation Religioethnic identity and self-fulfillment	Entrepreneurship Job opportunities Attending school
	A	B
	C	D
Others	Family unity Spouse's desire to return to homeland Alienated family head	Medical service personnel Educational service personnel

typology allows a comparison of the very different motives of Americans who moved to Australia—the Yanks—and those who went to Israel—the Olim.[4]

QUADRANT A SELF-EXPRESSIVE: ALIENATION, ADVENTURE, AND IDENTITY

One important cluster of motivations involved the search for personal fulfillment and meaning in life. The focus was usually more upbeat than simply "alienation," and not often as romantic as "pioneering." These Americans were seeking to fulfill their own personal emotional needs rather than to achieve specific goals. They were not necessarily loners, for many were accompanied by spouses and children. Husbands and wives usually had an equally strong desire to migrate and for the same reasons: to escape, to enhance a sense of identity and spirituality, and to see the world while they had the chance.

The Yanks in Australia: The Settlers

Most Americans explained their reasons for moving to Australia in terms of adventure and love of travel. While some form of social alienation pushed a minority to leave the United States, the major motivation was the pull of the host country's charms or the rewards of travel itself whatever the destination. But some settlers (that is, those who intended to stay for good) really were the alienated Americans who had generated some publicity in the press in the 1970s. However, they were not easy to find.

We looked hard in Melbourne for Americans who arrived thinking that they would stay. The first eight interviews were with Yanks who arrived intending to return to America. The ninth respondent was the first to say she knew that she had come for good, because her English husband's career was firmly tied to Australia. (This, however, was not a self-expressive focus.) Overall, 17 of the 50 personal interviews (34%) involved people (sometimes all the members of a family) who arrived as settlers. Similarly about one third of the survey respondents (35%) considered themselves settlers on arrival.

Although they all planned to stay permanently, the settlers we studied had many reasons for moving to Australia. Many were retirees, entrepreneurs, spouses of Australians, and dependents of people who intended to stay. Some wanted to establish for themselves new lives in Australia, and leave their problems back home. Some settlers had no particular love for Australia, others

[4]Working independently, Haour-Knipe (1990) studied 42 North American emigrants in Geneva, Switzerland, and found a similar set of motivations to which she attached different labels but similar distinctions. Her findings offer support for the distinctions proposed here.

extolled its advantages. Some bitterly criticized the "quality of life" as Finifter and Finifter (1980b) refer to it back in America. Others were unabashedly home-sick and patriotic Americans. Some had reached their decisions to stay amid feelings of demoralization, anxiety, outrage, and desperation. But most decisions were driven by love, loyalty, ambition, and adventure. Of course, people usually acted under the influence of various factors and emotions simultaneously, each changing in significance at different times. Overall, the patterns crystallized around the pull of family, the promise of profit, the discomfort of demoralization and the promise of peace of mind. Quadrant A includes all of these people.

People whom we call genuine settlers may be viewed as the ideal type of settlers. They seemed to conform to the model of migration that sees people as alienated from the "old world" and intent on starting new lives in another land. The genuine settlers were looking for a fresh start in life, for a sense of personal harmony. There was something, perhaps many things, that they wanted to leave far behind them: a humiliating experience; prolonged unemployment; the city; the crime; the crass materialism of their friends; the tensions and dangers of life in America; a sense of depression they just could not shake; a feeling that there had to be a better place to live and raise a family; or just some place where they could be unique and unknown, and so start life anew. We interviewed 26 people in Australia before we found the first prototypical genuine settler. Eventually we interviewed six people who felt alienated from their old way of life and wanted something they felt only Australia could offer. Ellen (the 27th interview) and her family are in many ways representative of these people:

> My husband was in the real estate business, and it was right during the time when everybody was going broke because they couldn't finance their business in 1971. They were looking for a loan and this money market was just completely dry. So his business went kaput. But at the same time all this was going on, for the 2 or 3 years before that, even though we were economically well off, it was a strange sort of atmosphere. You begin to think, "what am I doing here?" You go to a cocktail party, and people just talk about how many cars they have got, where their kids are going to school, and how much money they make, how many wigs they had. It was getting so bad. I just got to thinking, "this is a stupid way to live." It began gnawing at me. And we lived across from a university, and there was all this student unrest. This kept going on and every day on television it kept getting worse and worse and worse. And so when Marty's business failed, he started looking around for another job. The more he looked, the more we decided, "forget it." And then about three or four months before we could leave, Marty got an offer for a job in Atlanta working for one of the biggest department stores in Atlanta. They had a shopping center going up and they needed a manager. He turned it down quick smart, which really set in our minds that really we weren't going for any economic reasons, because otherwise he would've taken that offer. It really crystallized our thinking as to why we were coming. I suppose if the business hadn't failed, we would have just gone along, I don't know for how many years. Maybe sooner or later we would have just gotten fed up with all that. I suppose that pushed a situation that may not have come about.

Ellen spoke of alienation emerging from a personal economic crisis, eventually becoming a larger crisis of morale. Their best hope seemed to lie in escape, and they planned their move well (despite the typical problem of finding adequate information). The sense of personal insecurity matured into a "radical critique" of their society. As they looked deeper at America, the personal problem of work seemed to them to reflect a general social malaise. When work was finally found, they had already put too much psychological distance between themselves and their society, and Marty turned down the job. Their standard of living dropped sharply when they moved, from an American income of $25,000 (when the business had prospered in 1969) to an Australian income of $15,000 (the two countries had roughly equivalent costs of living in 1975). Although Americans usually experienced lower salary scales than in the States, most found their standard of living comparable to or better than in America: 27% of the surveyed respondents said their standard of living was better in Australia, 46% said it was about the same, and 24% said it was worse. Ellen and Marty did not consider this drop in earnings as a serious problem, saying they felt that their standard of living was comfortable in Australia.

Perhaps the most alienated Yank interviewed was Jim, who began by saying:

> We were concerned with the racial problem in the States, the drug problem, and the crime problem, and we felt like there had to be a better place in the world to bring children up, since we had three children. We decided we had to narrow it down to English-speaking countries. I'm too old (45) to try to learn another language. And so we narrowed it down to Australia and New Zealand, and we came over here to see if life could be more of what we thought it should be. So that's why we came over.

For Jim and his wife, Della, a growing sense of threat and unease with their lives in Miami erupted into virtual rebellion when they learned their three daughters would be bused to school in a black neighborhood thought to be dangerous. America had let them down.

Tony was a successful advertising executive in New York City, deeply resentful that he had been forced to sacrifice his ambition of becoming an actor in order to earn a living. He never quite got over that, and grew to hate the "rat race" of working in the big city. He might have gone to Hawaii, he said, but the employment situation there was terrible, and the cost of living was far too high. So, with a South Pacific dream, he systematically looked into Australia, mostly because he had some Australian friends where he lived. He moved in 1965. Soon after arriving, he found work as a cement mixer ("unlike anything I'd ever done before, but I survived; even got good at it"). Eventually he worked his way into television production. He went alone, but married an Australian woman he met on the voyage.

Sue and Roland married shortly after graduating from high school, and soon began thinking about migrating to Australia. Roland said he had always been the family's black sheep, and did not seem to fit in with most people. They talked about the smog of Southern California, the beaches being fenced in, and the difficulty of finding a job (Roland is a welder) in the States. His beard, their clothing, their casual life-style—all were reminiscent of hippies stranded in the 1970s. Not yet 20 when they moved, they were younger and less educated than most who decided to settle.

Steve would not say exactly what had happened, but ten years earlier his West Coast advertising agency had collapsed. He lost face, his friends deserted him, and he saw no hope for recovery. So he promptly moved to Australia. He spoke of a competitive system that would not "allow failure."

The last alienated American was Ed. He had lived in Hollywood with his Australian wife, Cass, before they moved to Australia. As he tells it, he was an alcoholic, brought on by the pressures and "phoniness" of the entertainment business. If he had stayed there, he thinks it would have killed him. So at the invitation of his Australian father-in-law, they sold everything, including their house, and moved to Melbourne:

> In Hollywood you had to have a new car every year, and you had to do this and do that, and keep up with the Joneses, especially in my profession. And everybody in Hollywood, it seemed, was living over their income. Believe me, they do. I've got a 5-year-old car, Ford Fairmont, running beautifully. Why buy a new car? Couldn't do that in America. Had to have a new car. And it had to be either a Lincoln or a Cadillac or an Oldsmobile. When you were making that kind of money, you had to show people you were making that kind of money. I made up my mind, burned all my bridges. I finished all my commitments, sold my car, sold my home, sold everything.

The genuine settlers were indeed the alienated Americans we expected to find. Most were so estranged from America that they felt they no longer belonged there. Some made carefully reasoned decisions, most were naive about what they might find, and a few made their decisions rather precipitously. The genuine settlers, however, were not the typical emigrant. To find out how many Americans felt that alienation was a significant factor in their move to Australia, the survey asked respondents to indicate the importance of each of a series of reasons for leaving the United States.

One out of four said that America's social problems were important in making their migration decisions, while half said this was not an important consideration. None of the other "alienation" responses was nearly as important as this one, and each was rejected by 3 to 1 margins or more. However, as we shall soon discuss, "desire for life in another country/travel/adventure" was the most popular reason of all: more than half (53%) said this was important (but 1 out of 7 rejected it).

We wondered if settlers were more likely than sojourners to cite social problems as factors in their decisions to leave the States. Settlers were indeed more likely than sojourners to point to the importance of America's social problems, but only by a slight margin (34% to 28%). On the other hand, settlers were more likely to consider this as unimportant (48%) compared to important (34%). Sojourners were even more likely to reject this as a decision factor, 62% (not important) to 28% (important). We estimate that one out of three settlers arrived as genuine settlers, alienated in some way from life in America. Overall, perhaps 10% to 15% of Americans who arrived in Australia with Permanent Residence Visas were the alienated Yanks who had captured so much public attention.[5]

The alienated dissolved their already weakened communal and family bonds. More frequently voiced for other settlers was the importance of maintaining social ties, not disrupting them, as we shall see. And just as important was the sheer pleasure of travel abroad. Americans were a much happier group of people than anyone had imagined. The sojourners, looking for a working holiday, are also found in quadrant A.

The Sojourners

Most Yanks who went to Australia holding Permanent Resident Visas did not intend to stay permanently at all. At least two thirds were sojourners, who believed they would someday return to the States, having fulfilled their yearning for travel and adventure. When asked why they left America for Australia, the majority (53%) of surveyed respondents replied that "desire for experience of life in another country/travel/adventure" was particularly important. Half of all respondents said that "escaping American social problems such as drug abuse or race" was not important, while 25% said it was. It would seem, then, that the adventure/travel motive should receive particular attention in any explanation of American migration to Australia. At least four other studies have revealed its importance, although they do not always attribute much significance to it (Finifter and Finifter, 1980b; Australian Department of Labour and Immigration, 1969; Bardo and Bardo, 1980c; Cuddy, 1977).

Why, then, did they secure Permanent Resident Visas? Because this gave them flexibility in setting their return schedules and permitted them to find work

[5]The Australian Department of Labour and Immigration study (1969, 1971) reported that 29% said that the desire for travel was the main reason for migrating, the highest response of any category (followed by employment opportunities, 21%; all family-related reasons combined, 17%; and escape from social tensions, 14%). The report's conclusions, however, largely ignore this finding and discuss only those Americans who prefer living in Australia for reasons other than economic advantage. Finifter and Finifter (1980a), as part of their focus on the values and political orientations of American migrants (see 1980b, 1982), found adventure/travel to be an important motive. Despite the large percentage of responses in this category (nearly equal to "economic betterment"), they consider this relatively unimportant, concluding that the travel and adventure motives did not possess universal significance. Interestingly, they attribute more importance to what they term the "quality of life" motive, despite the significantly fewer responses in this category compared with "travel and adventure." Finally, Cuddy (1977) also ignored the adventure/travel motive. More than 55% of his respondents selected "for adventure" as their prime motive for migrating, the single most popular response. Nonetheless, he dismissed the finding, instead focusing on the far fewer (26%) responses to the category "becoming overcrowded" (see DeAmicis, 1980).

in Australia. The Australians call this a "working holiday," a chance to finance an overseas adventure with a job in that country. Some said they would return in six months or that their contract stipulated two or three years (usually with return passage paid by the employer). But sometimes there was no real time limit, no need to go right back, not yet. After all, the point was to satisfy a sense of wanderlust, to experience a foreign land, and not to achieve a tangible goal. Who could tell how long it would take to satisfy the spirit? Here is how one sojourner, Gail, 28, single, a teacher, and a four-year resident of Australia, explained her intent:

> I thought I would come over for two years on Assisted Passage and give it a go. I filled out all the papers for Assisted Passage, which meant at least two years. And then I just thought I'd play it by ear from there. . . . When most people ask "how long are you going to stay here?" I reply, "until I get tired."

Bob was 35, a clergyman, married to an Australian woman, and an 11-year resident in Australia. When asked, "did you think you would stay here?", Bob replied:

> No, I didn't think that. I had no plans to stay, but again, it's pretty vague. Just existential type of existence, what seems good at the time is what you do. The future will sort itself out.

It was characteristic of these self-expressive Yanks that they were young adults, college-educated, childless, and unencumbered by commitments of home ownership, community involvement, or career. Their goals were diffuse. They expected to find work when they arrived, which is why they acquired Permanent Resident Visas. Although loosely integrated into their native American society, they could not be considered alienated or estranged from it. Indeed, they were activated by the basic American values of travel and cosmopolitan experiences.

Many stayed longer than they had anticipated, and we shall examine later how some sojourners became progressively integrated into Australian life. But most returned to America as originally planned, not out of rejection of Australia, but because they had satisfied their thirst for adventure and it was time to go home. Another group of sojourners, who arrived with more specific goals in mind, were more likely to become permanent residents. We shall find them in quadrant B.

The Olim

Clear differences emerge in comparing the motivation of the Australian and Israeli groups. While the motives of Americans migrating to Australia tend to be more privatized, even "hedonistic," the motives of Americans migrating to Israel (who grew up in religioethnic subcommunities) seem to be more ethnicized or collectivized. To some degree, the motivations of the Israeli-bound group can be considered somewhat "altruistic" (in Durkheim's terminology) inasmuch as the migrants refer to their role within the framework of the Jewish people.[6] They seek to ensure the continuity of the group although, as a matter of course, this has an impact on their own personal lives. As one university professor stated:

> We had long-range problems with the children: the fact that they would be living in a non-Jewish country and in a non-Jewish overall environment where they would be the minority . . . where the cultural and religious values tended to weigh in favor of Christian values.

Clearly these immigrants were not moving to Israel to increase their personal fortunes. In almost all cases the standard of living of these immigrants was lower in Israel than it would have been had they remained in the United States. On the contrary, some of the migrants wanted to get away from a life centered on economic achievement. "I felt life (in the United States) was terribly materialistic—meaning everything in terms of money," said one female settler.

We found a general theme of dissatisfaction with life in the American Jewish community. "Overall the American Jewish community was doomed; there was no future . . . not for our children. It was on the road to assimilation," stated one of the females. "Jewishness was reading a Jewish novel or going to a Jewish restaurant that served cheesecake," said another. Two of the males stated that "many Jews took American values and called them Jewish, and in a sense they did not know Jewish tradition. Take the Golden Rule, and accept the Christian wording rather than the Jewish." The other said, "A lot of their commitment to Jewishness, or Jewish peoplehood, is quite shallow, and they're not doing a very effective job about passing it on to the next generation." In sum, said yet another male, "we weren't fulfilled as Jews in the Jewish community."

These migrants were pulled in search of a better Jewish life rather than pushed from America, and Israel represented the focus of their Jewish yearning and motivations. Both Berman (1979) and Goldscheider (1974) reported similar findings in earlier studies. Although their frames of references were frequently religious, it was not necessarily in a traditional Orthodox Jewish sense. They were alienated more from Jewish life in America and the limitations of minority group status than from American political institutions. For example, only 40% of the premigrant group we studied were satisfied with Jewish religious services in America.

[6]Durkheim (1951, p. 221) distinguished between "egoistic" and "altruistic" in his analysis of suicide in this manner:

> Having given the name of *egoism* to the state of ego living its own life and obeying itself alone, that of *altruism* adequately expresses the opposite state, where the ego is not its own property, where it is blended with something not itself, where the goal of conduct is exterior to itself, that is, in one of the groups in which it participates.

This definition seems to also aptly describe the difference between emigration to Israel and Australia.

"You belonged to a synagogue . . . because that was the thing to do, where you met the people that were important to you socially or business-wise," said one of the Olim when criticizing the nature of religious life in the United States. Disillusionment with the clergy was expressed by a different respondent who stated that "the rabbinate, of all the trends, is bankrupt as far as showing leadership." Just 31% of the premigration group were satisfied with Jewish educational opportunities for their children. Correspondingly, one Oleh reported: "We weren't fulfilled as Jews in the American Jewish community. We couldn't bring up the children there." Finally, only 29% of the premigrant sample were satisfied with Jewish organizational life. As one of the Olim put it: "I resented the leadership of the community being taken over by people . . . whose success was purely monetary. Intellectual values didn't count for anything."

Likewise, the migrants studied in the Israel Immigrant Absorption Survey were found to be more Jewishly identified than American Jews as a whole. For example, 28% of the migrants were Orthodox (compared to the 1971 National Jewish Population Survey figure of 11%); 29% had an intensive Jewish education in a day school (compared to 4% in 1971 of all American Jews); and 29% of the migrants reported going to synagogue once a week or more (compared to just 8% in 1971 of all U.S. Jews). Indeed, Americans who joined the Conservative and Reform movements in Israel observed much more ritual than their counterparts in the United States. They even observed more ritual practices on the average than Israeli Jews (Tabory and Lazerwitz, 1983).

Other researchers have reported similar findings. Avruch (1981), for example, argues that the question of the motivation of migration of U.S. Jews to Israel relates to their Jewish identity. The fundamental question is why Israel is chosen as the land of immigration. Avruch (p. 93) notes that even when objective reasons are given with regard to the push factors, such as the undesirability of raising a family in the United States or drug problems, the reasons given for going to Israel are phrased in subjective terms. People in Israel "feel at home" and "belong." Avruch (p. 94) explains the difference between objective and subjective critiques of American life in the following way: The objective critics say that they did not like America because of what it was. The subjective critics did not like America because of what it was and because of what they were, or because of what their children would become.

The Pull of Enhancement

Although the push of estrangement and the pull of adventure were present to some extent among the migrants to Israel, it was far more typical of emigration to Israel to revolve about the pull of enhancement of life opportunities in the spiritual realm. The evidence presented is drawn from the premigration sample of those preparing to live in Israel (the premigrants) as well as the migration group already living there. Goldberg (1985), who similarly studied American Jews' readiness to consider emigrating to Israel, reported that a strong Jewish identity was the main pull factor.

While 48% of the premigrants praised the feeling of closeness and togetherness among American Jews, a closer analysis revealed a lack of substantial satisfaction in several specific areas. Only 40% were "a lot satisfied" with religious services and less were similarly satisfied with Jewish education for their children (31%), Zionist groups (29%), and Jewish organizations (29%).

A 20-year-old male college student who was planning to live in Israel in about two years after the interview stated the following about Jewish education:

> I think it's incredibly poor . . . believe it or not. I went to school for six years, and I was taught basically little or nothing about the Holocaust and Israel, perhaps some of the greatest phenomena in Jewish history today. I think it's very sad.

Perhaps a clue to this lack of substantial satisfaction with American Jewry lies in the fact that a little more than one half of the premigrants (54%) reported that what they liked least about American Jewry was its "apathy." As a 29-year-old male who planned to live on a kibbutz said:

> Their complete apathy and lip service as far as Israel is concerned . . . there is no such thing as a Zionist group in America, Zionists live in Israel, not America, and 99% of the people who are part of the Zionist group never make aliya, never even think about making aliya, to them it's like . . . a little club or a bingo thing that happens once a week . . . the true Zionist lives in Israel not in America.

Another possible source of dissatisfaction was the contact with the larger Gentile society. The overwhelming majority of the premigrants (86%) reported having close non-Jewish friends. While two thirds (67%) of the respondents reported that they could share their feelings with their non-Jewish friends and felt no gap separated them, more than half (54%) reported they felt they had problems living in American society at times such as Christmas.

Similarly, a typical comment of American immigrants surveyed in Israel concerning this question was:

> I didn't like (the Christmas period). I felt annoyed, irritated that I should be subjected to several weeks of the constant feeling of Christmas. At work everyone said to each other "Merry Christmas." The Jews said to each other "Merry Christmas." In all aspects one feels that one is living in a Christian country.

Indeed, approximately one quarter (28%) of those preparing to live in Israel reported that they felt that Jews were a minority group who were discriminated against. An extreme comment by an American in Israel, in this regard, was "It's just a matter of time. If you live in *Golus* (exile), it's a matter of time until you have to leave the country anyway." Similarly, another said, "Christianity represents to us a hostile force. The Gentile is always a potential enemy, no matter how friendly he is."

A similar 28% of those preparing to live in Israel also reported that they felt that America was basically a Christian society. A 26-year-old single male with a bachelor's degree who was preparing to move to Israel put it this way:

> They (Christians) seemed to be associating Communism and Jews . . . with something dangerous . . . there was a fear of something, a prejudice of some kind lurking in there. I tend just to think that as Christians they have somewhat of a guilt complex about the way Jews have been persecuted. They're horrified by the Holocaust.

Finally, a university professor, interviewed after his immigration, reported:

> I was always uncomfortable; no—change the word to—unhappy—that I was living in a Christian country. Its values were in some way being—not forced upon me since I could resist them—but forced in front of me.

Despite the fact that a clear majority (63%) reported that they felt fully part of the total American society, a similar majority (62%) indicated that they felt more Jewish than American. Only 12 of 49 Americans interviewed in Israel stated that they had felt completely part of American society prior to immigration (Tabory, 1975). While it is possible to attribute the differences of the studies to the time of the survey or the sampling frame, it is possible that one is more aware of how distant one was from involvement in the total society when such an analysis is made after migration.

What emerges from these data is a picture of a group of people who were highly identified as Jews and felt a part of American society as a whole. Nevertheless, a majority expressed certain specific areas of discomfort as American Jews, for example, the problem of coping with the pervasiveness of Christmas celebration and a lack of substantial satisfaction with existing Jewish organizations, Zionist groups, and the kind of Jewish education available for children. This made them responsive to emigration.

A high level of Jewish identification alone might not lead American Jews to move to Israel given the simple fact that many American Jews are clearly highly identified, such as rabbis and other "professional Jews," but they continue to live in the United States. A sense of some estrangement from American society in general or from American Jewry's institutions in particular is likely to make such Jews feel less integrated. But these factors might not be enough without some contact with the Israeli experience to suggest an alternative way of life.

Among the premigrants such experience was very evident. Nearly two thirds (66%) reported that they had Israeli friends, and the same percent reported that they had close relatives living in Israel (most since 1967). Moreover, the overwhelming majority (89%) had visited Israel. This compared to National Jewish Population Survey data that showed by 1971 that only 16% of American Jews had visited Israel and only 30% intended to do so. Indeed, for the premigrants, 64% reported they had visited Israel more than once (most for at least one month). Only about one third (34%) were involved in the Association of

Americans and Canadians for Aliya, or AACA (now known as NAAM, North American Aliya Movement), which sponsors groups or clubs for premigrants, but close to one half (43%) expressed a good deal of familiarity with life in Israel.

Interestingly enough, the respondents did not expect to be any more satisfied in terms of religious services in Israel or by Zionist groups there. (Only 37% expected a lot of satisfaction in terms of religious groups and just 28% in terms of Zionist groups.) In one area, however, people expected a lot more satisfaction: 69% of the respondents reported that they expected a lot of satisfaction in Jewish education for their present or future children. Thus, the majority of persons (65%) in the premigrant group were pulled to Israel, and the opportunity for a better Jewish education for their children stood out as one highly attractive feature.

The great majority of the premigrants (71%) expected that their standard of living would decrease. The result would be, according to nearly one half the respondents (46%), a need to sacrifice materially the luxuries to which they had been accustomed. For only a few was the loss of a car (11%) or money (14%) seen as a great sacrifice. Of all the responses given to the question as to what would be the greatest noneconomic sacrifice due to migration, the most frequent one was loss of family and friendship ties with 69% of respondents reporting this.

Perhaps the economic and kinship losses would be offset by the perceived gain and adventure of living in Israeli society. Respondents reported they expected less crime than in American society (86%), better public transportation (83%), and better schools (40%).

In the area of political and social beliefs, the premigrants tended toward a liberal approach with respect to political and social issues. A majority or plurality wanted the Israeli (Labor) government to do more to encourage the opening of non-Orthodox congregations (74%), permit civil marriage (54%), narrow the Israeli social and economic gap (49%), and to permit constituency elections to the Knesset (45%). Only in two areas probed did the respondents believe the government was moving along "about right" so that the status quo was acceptable: to reach a peace agreement with the Arabs (63%) and to restrict buses on the Sabbath (54%).

These beliefs did not translate, however, into clear-cut support or opposition for a political party in Israel. Indeed, 71% did not have a preference for an Israeli political party. Of those who did, the preference was toward the left with 23% of all respondents preferring one of the Labor political factions. It is, therefore, not surprising that a majority of respondents (54%) identified themselves as political liberals. This political liberalism was reflected in a concern for more economic, political, and religious opportunity in Israeli society. As the 20-year-old college student mused about life in America:

> I'm not exactly *pleased* with the environment I live in. If I was truly dedicated as a
> Socialist, I would work towards changing here; but the fact is I'm a Zionist and as a
> result I don't think I could even stay here.

Judaism, combined with some measure of Zionism, clearly affects most of the migrants who move to Israel. Antonovsky (1968) found that 7% of his respondents listed religious reasons as a primary motivating factor in their migration. Just a few years later Jubas (1974) found that 23% of the migrants that he studied indicated this as a primary reason. Having said this, we should note that there are some ultra-Orthodox Jewish migrants who come only because of their belief in Israel as the Holy Land where one can most properly observe God's commandments. Some of these persons do not even accept the secular authority of the state and believe that Israel transgresses in trying to supplant the Messiah in bringing redemption to the land. Their feeling is that God will protect and take care of them, no matter how difficult their economic and political situation might be. Essentially, these persons belong to the relatively small ultra-Orthodox *Haredi* movement, and they view the state as an extension of the Jewish community rather than as a civil entity (Liebman, 1988). They are not particularly liked by either religious or Jewish secular Israeli Jews (Cohen, 1988). The number of persons who hold these extreme views is small, but it is a qualitatively interesting group as far as their motivation for migration.

In conclusion, in their own minds the major reason for emigration to Israel among the respondents was their Jewish identification and their view of Israel as the homeland of the Jewish people. Seven out of ten premigrants reported this as their reason for emigration. Despite the widespread feeling of loyalty to Israel as the Jewish home, only 34% reported they were making aliya in two years or less and only 48% in five years or less. Thus, about half of this group who were considering migration had rather vague and distant plans for emigration. Similarly, about one half (49%) rated their probability of returning to America subsequently as more than 50–50. Among the sample of Americans living in Israel, 61% reported that Israel offered the main opportunity to live a more complete Jewish life, and only a fraction (2%) rated their probability of returning as more than 50–50.

Before concluding this section, we present the case of Dan, a young, successful American Jew who had done very well for himself in California, to illustrate how a person who could have been identified as a sojourner and an entrepreneur in Israel is nevertheless affected by a collective-ethnic orientation.

Dan had become wealthy at an early age and he owned a chain of home product stores. Single, he was most devoted to his Persian carpets and swimming pool and to his summer house in Mexico. He even carried pictures of them around in his wallet. Nevertheless, seeking something more stimulating than opening another set of stores, he decided to take a year off and tour the world.

His travels brought him to Egypt from where he planned to continue on to

India. A series of storms in India, however, left him with time until he could depart for his continued wanderings. He decided to travel north for a short visit to Israel.

Dan had received some Jewish education as a child, but religion had not meant much to him. However, once in Israel he felt right at home. His outgoing personality led him to make friends very quickly. He decided to stay a little bit longer. Being an entrepreneur, he thought, why not make a little money as long as he was there? It did not really matter that he had a tourist visa that did not allow him to work. That was only a technical issue.

Dan started by working as a realty agent. It was a natural beginning, since he had to find a place for himself to live anyway. After a while he realized that he could do much better by working for himself. He also met and eventually married an Israeli woman. Dan was in Israel to stay. His motivation?

> Well, here the people are all me. I mean being Jewish wasn't so important for me, and I'm not at all observant. But being with Jews all the time, I mean you realize that you are close to even people who you aren't close to. I didn't have a feeling like that before.

Dan is not a "born-again" Zionist, though.

> To go back? Who knows? Just because I have an oleh visa now doesn't mean I'm here to stay. It depends how things go. My wife and I could take our daughter anywhere and manage.

Overall, these data seem to suggest that the commitment to emigration to Israel even among those seriously considering it is not overwhelming. For some, perhaps, it is fraught with fear of the unknown, for some with family conflicts, and for some it is a dream of a lifetime and the expectation of a lifestyle to be realized, perhaps at retirement. Careful examination should be made of what happens to the commitment of those who eventually do emigrate. Does their commitment increase or decrease? What effect does it have on their remaining or returning to America? These questions will be addressed in Chapters 6 and 7.

Perhaps the decision to emigrate should not be seen as final. Rather, the decision may be the result of a delicate balance of decision making that shifts back and forth as different weights enter the scale of decisions to be made. In this way emigration need not necessarily mean that one has severed all ties and will not return to America.

SUMMARY

In this chapter we began our analysis of the similarities and differences in the cross-national comparison of Americans who have emigrated to Australia (the Yanks) and those who went to Israel (the Olim). In comparing these two groups, we found them to be similar in a variety of biosocial characteristics: age, marital status, level of formal education, and employment. While they held these characteristics in common, they diverged from the general adult American population in that they were much younger, slightly less likely to be married, more highly educated, and more likely to be professionally employed. Only in one area for which data were available was there a difference between the groups, and that was sex. Slightly less than three fifths of the surveyed Americans in Israel were female, but exactly three fifths of those surveyed in Australia were male.

In examining the motivation for migration we first defined *international migration* as the voluntary and permanent relocation from one country to another for more than one year. In developing a framework for analyzing motivations we constructed a table which arrayed the *locus of concern* (self or others) on the vertical axis against the horizontal *goals of migration* (expressive or instrumental). This yielded four quadrants. In *quadrant A*, the migrant's focus is *self-expressive*, for example, fulfillment of one's religioethnic identity. In *quadrant B*, the orientation is *self-instrumental*, as in achieving a personal, external good, such as starting a business. In *quadrant C*, the direction is *others-expressive* activities, such as emigrating after marrying someone from the adopted country. In *quadrant D*, the emphasis is on *others-instrumental*, which includes those who migrated to serve as medical or educational service personnel.

The remainder of the chapter was devoted to fleshing out the detailed motivations presented in quadrant A. Here we saw that the primary motivations for Americans emigrating to Australia was the search for adventure, travel, or a working holiday; and for emigration to Israel, the quest was for expanding the meaning of one's religioethnic identity.

At this point we may note that the findings reported in this chapter are consistent with our contention that the motivation for migration for these migrants is best explained on the social psychological level. It is not an entire class of a specific type of persons that emigrate, nor are the persons who move composed only of individuals who have no common denominator. Rather, it is a combination of the ways in which a certain group of individuals react to the social environment that has an impact on the decision to move.

4

More on Motives

In this chapter we examine the variety of motivations arrayed in quadrants B (self-instrumental), C (others-expressive), and D (others-instrumental) for which data are available. We begin with the self-instrumental motivations. "Well, do you ever find yourself asking why you have stayed here for 7 years?" asked the interviewer:

> Oh, yes, and I think the main reason is economical, and because Dick isn't really that keen to leave. We can't go to England because of the economic situation there. And he doesn't feel that he can go to America, and I couldn't get a job teaching in America at the moment either, because there's a glut.

Thus spoke Chris who had lived in Australia for seven years, although she had intended to stay only a year or two when she arrived. But then she had not intended to marry Dick, an Englishman and commercial artist, when she moved there.

QUADRANT B SELF-INSTRUMENTAL

Quadrant B, the self-instrumental objective, includes that cluster of motives that focus on migration as a means to achieve tangible, personally important goals. The intent is not necessarily permanent settlement in and of itself, as it was for example, with the alienated Yanks. For once an instrumental goal is reached, it may cease to be a motivating factor. More frequently, the traveler intends to achieve a limited end. In the case of the Yanks in Australia, the goals range from the relatively "settling" intention of starting a business, to working in a prearranged job for a year or two, to retrieving a war-stranded bride. In each case, the destination, Australia, is incidental to the larger end. And again, for most Yanks, migration does not imply a commitment to settle. The entrepreneurs are the exception. They knew they would stay for good.

Entrepreneurs

Entrepreneurs were people who migrated to start new businesses. One way or another, they perceived opportunities to exploit untapped markets. Some were already familiar with Australia before making their investment. Surprisingly, a few went into it almost impulsively. But all of them decided to move to Australia because that was where the opportunity lay. Harry, an income tax consultant, explains:

> We came with the understanding that we're going to run this business, we're going to live here, enjoy ourselves, fit in with the community—I suppose in that order. . . . I sort of looked at it as investing a few years to have the rewards that would come later. But I could have said that about Phoenix, or New York City, or Calgary. This happened in Melbourne because there was nobody else wanting the job.

Altogether, we interviewed four entrepreneurs in Australia. Alan had an idea for a chain of restaurants (which is how we came across his name. Australians frequently urged us to "go talk with Alan; he owns that restaurant in Melbourne.") His excited manner and rapid-fire speech contrasted with Mark's slow, careful conversation. Mark's life as a world-traveling representative for an American multinational corporation had often brought him to Australia, where he thought he saw a market for pork, "if you can make it taste right." And David felt he could help start a whole new industry by growing and processing cotton. David brought a large family; Mark, his children full grown, was accompanied by only his wife; Alan came alone, leaving a recently divorced wife and several children behind. All assumed that if they wanted their businesses to succeed, they would have to be ready to live there a long time, perhaps the rest of their lives. They all liked Australia well enough to make this choice. But it was the investment opportunities that brought them, more than an attraction for the country. None felt "pushed" by alienation from their homeland. Three of them seemed to have been moderately successful in their careers in the States, but felt "restless" rather than alienated.

To see how many other Americans migrated principally as entrepreneurs, the survey asked, "Were any of the following circumstances especially involved in your coming to Australia?" Of the variety of responses elicited by the question, about 14% of the settlers and as many as 8% of all respondents came to start a business. Each was probably influenced by several factors at once as they made their decisions to permanently relocate. Harry and Mary were bored with their business's success, and their decision seemed almost impulsive. Alan was "looking for the sun," as he put it, and a week's visit to Sydney convinced him that this was the place to start a chain of restaurants. Restless, confident, almost brash, he described it as something of a madcap adventure. Mark, on the other hand, after years of literally worldwide research, thought Australia was the ideal place to invest his nest egg. With retirement in sight, he took great care to invest wisely.

David's difficulty in expanding his California farm (due to the price of land) provoked an urge "to get away from it all." So, entrepreneurs had more than just business on their mind. They spoke with words such as "challenge," "opportunity," "rewards," and "investment."

One study has mentioned entrepreneurs as a significant group of migrating Americans. Finifter and Finifter believe that many of the self-employed in their survey of American emigrants to Australia arrived to start a business. Noting the large percentage of self-employed Americans, they explain: "Apart from the apparent greater opportunity for self-employment in Australia, this pattern may also reflect a strong entrepreneurial spirit among Americans who migrate to Australia" (Finifter and Finifter, 1980a, p. 5). However, their data suggest that as many as 18% of their respondents could be entrepreneurs.

The entrepreneurs did not see their decisions as irrevocable. Living in Australia was pleasant enough, but they could be attracted by an even better investment opportunity elsewhere. It did not seem likely, but it could happen. In this respect they differed from people in the genuine settler category, who had made an irrevocable decision and intended to make a whole new life.

Working Holidays

Many Yanks went to Australia with prearranged jobs awaiting them, but permanent settlement was hardly their aim. Accepting a job in Australia was usually a limited affair; a contract for two years, as in the case of American teachers and other professionals. For a few, this was just another assignment by the parent company, who could transfer them at a moment's notice. Those who went as contract workers typically were lured as well by the thrill of travel and the prospect of living abroad for a few years, with the income (and often the airfare over and back) guaranteed. Such a job could also provide occupational security for the unemployed or career enhancement for those just getting started after graduating from college. The personal fulfillment of travel abroad would seem to place many of these people in quadrant A, just discussed. However, without a tangible job awaiting them, they would not have gone to Australia. It was employment that drew them there.

Overall, one of the most common circumstances bringing Americans to Australia was employment as contracted workers. The Australian education system had been particularly active in recruiting Americans for secondary school and university positions (Bardo and Bardo, 1980a, estimate that there were more than 1,200 in the state of Victoria alone in 1977). Australian private industry also frequently solicited American talent. We interviewed people recruited by Australian advertising agencies, swimming pool contractors, engineering firms, the Protestant ministry, and graphic design studios. The terms of recruitment generally provided transportation for the entire family to and from Australia. Sometimes the contract could be renewed, which usually included an expense-paid visit back to the States before beginning another period of work. When this research was undertaken in Australia in 1974, there were many Yanks in the Australian secondary school system. Americans who were recent college graduates without entry-level jobs in the States looked forward to going to Australia for a two-year stint (or, some thought, perhaps a little longer). Like Scott and Pat below, they were attracted by the promise of a foreign adventure. But it was the valuable job experience that drew them to Australia. Their eventual goal was to return to the States to teach in high school.

We interviewed Scott and Pat in their small, cozy, modern, furnished flat in a middle-income neighborhood. They had been in Melbourne for three years, which was one year longer than originally planned. They were now looking for a house to buy. Scott taught at a nearby secondary school, where Pat also worked as a librarian.

We asked, "When was the first time you thought about leaving the States, not just for a trip, but for living or migrating?" Scott replied:

> Other than the "Tropical Island Syndrome," I can't think of any serious attempt. The first serious thing was when we were married and I was looking for a job, and this sort of sprung up. We were living at home in Oregon. We sort of saw a *Time* magazine article, that was what kicked it off. They had a big thing about Australia. I was looking for jobs and I wasn't getting anywhere. The job situation was pretty bleak. And I heard somebody mention something about needing teachers, so we started to apply.

People like Scott and Pat took advantage of an opportunity for foreign travel, adventure, and independence. College friends were scattering after graduation, employment prospects were poor, and they were determined to become independent from parents. They saw the Australian position as a good chance to make their start in life.

Julie was another West Coast resident who discovered this same kind of opportunity in the midst of her own personal crisis. She was 35 and had lived in Australia for four years. She and her two preschool children lived in a two-bedroom flat just two blocks from a lovely beach. She had divorced her husband shortly before leaving for Australia, and the experience had left her life in disarray. Now she had an Australian boyfriend whom she was considering marrying. She was deeply involved in her work as a teacher. At last she felt she had stabilized her life.

We asked her, "Can you recall when you first thought about migrating from the United States, even if it wasn't for Australia?" She answered:

> That's a very difficult question. I never really did. What I did was look for a job, a teaching job. I called the University of California job center and asked if they had any interviews, and they said "yes, we have an interview on Wednesday, as a matter of fact, for Australia." And my friend Jane advised me to take the interview, which I did. The idea of traveling to Australia, if they'd accept me with 2 children, especially when

I was divorced from my husband and looking for a full-time job, really appealed to me. I thought, "I always wanted to travel and this would be ideal." I could sort of have a working holiday. The idea of staying here occurred after I'd been here. But the idea of actually migrating just never crossed my mind. I had never worked full time during my marriage. I'd been a home-bound teacher, I did that part time, and ran my own tutoring service. And then after I was separated I began to substitute teach. And then I was offered a position in San Francisco, in P.E. (physical education) and English. But I don't do P.E. (physical education); but they said I could fake it; they'd give me the job—I knew somebody. Then I got this interview for Australia, I'd always been fascinated by Australia. I thought, "if they'll take me, what the hell, why not, for two years out of my life, fantastic, I'm going." I got the job and here I am.

The experiences of Scott and Pat and Julie are similar in many ways and reveal a good deal about many Americans recruited to work in Australia. They more or less stumbled onto the opportunity to go without having to pay for the trip. While none knew much of substance about Australia before deciding, all they really needed to know was that Australians speak English. Despite their lack of familiarity with the country, they felt they were risking little, since what little they did know (especially through social contacts with Australians) supported an assumption that Australia was not so different from the States. Since they did not intend to stay, they did not have to consider seriously such complications as family feelings, the distance from home, or friends left behind. With secure jobs awaiting them, they were relieved of the worry of earning a living. There were no heart-wrenching decisions, no cutting of family ties, no sense of turning their backs on their homes. There was also very little with respect to conventional obligations to keep them home, either. Overall, at least 22% of respondents noted the importance of work-related or study-related factors.

Many revealed personal problems that influenced their decisions to exploit these opportunities for travel and life abroad. These problems were often associated with work: unemployment, competition for recognition and advancement, narrowing employment choices, and lack of professional experience. Some mentioned the chance to broaden educational or professional experiences. Another frequently mentioned concern was deteriorating family relationships, often made worse by financial difficulties. And some could not quite put their finger on what was troubling them back in the States, but they knew they needed to get away from home for a while.

Two circumstances were repeatedly involved in such decisions. For one thing, these Americans were usually professionally trained and highly skilled. The teachers, for instance, all had college degrees. Americans have long been noted for being more highly educated than other migrant groups—more, in fact, than Australians and Americans in general. The bulk of the American migration took place at a time when Australia was rapidly expanding its social services as a result of the tremendous growth in its population due to post-World War II immigration. For example, universities were expanding and they sought the surplus of American Ph.D.'s to complete their staff. Furthermore, the recent growth of the television industry had spurred a demand for media professionals: advertising executives with up-to-date American know-how, production workers, and entertainers. American business acumen was heavily recruited by other Australian enterprises as well. Americans were well trained, under far more competitive conditions than in Australia, and had a reputation for working hard. So these people were equipped with particularly useful skills and training and represented a "reverse brain-drain" phenomenon. That is, instead of highly trained people being attracted to a country with a higher standard of living (the United States), they were going to a country with a lower standard of living (Australia).

Second, since they were generally in unstable, transitory stages in their life cycles, they were but weakly integrated into American society. Scott had recently graduated from college, just married, and was impatient for adult independence. Julie was divorced, struggling to survive, needing a secure job, and bickering with her family. Some came to do graduate work in a university. Two interviewees were trying to escape the draft. Others were just out of military service. Very few were firmly tied to stable careers, home ownership, or tight community involvement in the States. Once they had finished work in Australia, they would return to the States for "life as normal."

The reader will note that thus far emigrants to Israel have not been mentioned in this section. The reason for this is that not many of the Jews who moved to Israel appeared to do so for instrumental or economic reasons. Less than half of the 49 respondents in the Americans in Israel study had much knowledge about working conditions in Israel prior to their migration, and only five of them said that they enjoyed a higher standard of living in Israel as compared with the United States. (Two of those five enjoyed a higher standard of living because they were able to finally use the many tax-free purchases that they had saved up for prior to their migration and that they had never had in the United States.) One person said that he came to Israel because he had been turned down for a job in the United States, but he attributed the reason for that to anti-Semitism; and he consequently "wanted to get away from that type of society."

It is always difficult to substantiate a negative finding, and saying the migrants did not come because of instrumental reasons is a negative conclusion. Still, we note that almost all of the 49 interviewees felt that they had made economic sacrifices in moving to Israel. These included the inability to save money (12 persons), the inability to travel freely (10), and, in general, suffering from the mentality of being poor (14). Five persons mentioned the difficulty of having to buy apartments that from an American perspective were tremendously overpriced, and five persons mentioned the problem of having to pay much money to replace appliances that broke down. (This problem would probably be felt by the others at a later date when all their new appliances would start deteriorating. The cost of appliances in Israel is two to four times the cost of the same appliances in the United States.) A popular joke that veteran American immigrants in Israel enjoy telling is: How do you make a small fortune in Israel? By starting with a large one and watching it rapidly diminish!

This is not to say that Americans in Israel have not necessarily done well for themselves. The point is that the Americans who moved to Israel did so, by and large, despite the economic situation that they generally encountered. In this connection we note that earlier research conducted in Israel indicates that the basic motivation for migration appears not to have substantially changed over time. Antonovsky (1968) found that economic factors hardly played any role in his study of American migrants. The attraction of Israel and a pioneering spirit was found by him to be a primary motive for migration. Similarly, Jubas (1974) notes that the economic pull of "a better job or position in Israel" characterized only 3% of the American migrants that he studied. His survey of more than a thousand immigrants found that the main reason for motivation could be sum- marized in one word, "Jewishness." Moving to Israel because that is where the economic opportunities existed is not a primary motivation for this group of persons.

Having emphasized the ideological factors in the migration decision, we should note that we did encounter some religious Jews whose motivation for migration was affected by economic consideration to some degree. Parents of large families have told us that the much greater expense of intensive Jewish day school or yeshiva training in the United States relative to Israel was making it impossible for them to continue to give their children the type of education that they wanted. Hence, they thought they would be better able to finance such an education in Israel.

Romance

Another group of sojourners made their way to Australia without jobs awaiting them on arrival, without official sponsorship, and with no idea they would stay. They were men going back to visit a girlfriend or to get married. These Americans had been there before with the military, some during a ship's port of call, and others for up to a year or longer during World War II. A trip to Australia was intended to resolve a personal relationship, while they still had the chance before taking up "life as normal" back home. Visiting Australia was a necessary means to this end. Thus, "romance" fits into quadrant B, the self- instrumental cluster. Brian was one of these ex-servicemen.

Brian was 50 and lived in Australia more than 30 years. He was married to an Australian, and all four of their children were born there. He is a solicitor (as Australians call lawyers), and this had a great deal to do with why he stayed. He reluctantly became an Australian citizen in order to practice law. (None of the people quoted so far had changed citizenship.) We met with Brian in his home, a large and expensive house in a fashionable suburb of Melbourne. The hedge-enclosed backyard had a swimming pool. He earned enough per year to make him among the most affluent of Australians, American or otherwise. He felt he was completely Australianized, but even after 30 years his accent revealed his New York City origins.

We talked about his experiences and asked, "in October, 1945, you came back . . . did you come back to get your wife, or did you come back to stay?" He replied at length:

> Well, no, initially I came back to get my wife. It was easier for me to go to Australia than for her to get to the United States as an unmarried or engaged woman at the time. If she were already married, there would have been no difficulty. The initial reason was to return to Australia and marry her and return with my wife. And my father-in-law suggested that I stay in Australia, see if I liked it. If I didn't like it, well, then he would assist us to return to the United States. Well, I thought that was fair enough, and I decided I'd try a few things, looking around and seeing what I wanted to do. My mother-in-law heard I could do the GI Bill of Rights in Australia. I don't know how she heard, but I decided to investigate . . . I found I could go to the university and continue my studies under the GI Bill. And I decided that perhaps business was better suited to me than medicine because I didn't feel I could make a good doctor after seeing so many injured people in the war. So I started a course in commerce in Melbourne University. After 2 years of commerce, which has a good deal of law in it, I decided that I enjoyed law very much and determined to get both a commerce and law degree, which I did, concentrating more on commercial law than the other portion of the law.

All told, we interviewed seven Americans who first went to Australia with the military, five of them during World War II. Each said he had returned in order to resolve a romantic relationship established during the initial trip: to reunite with a wife stranded by the war, to consummate an engagement, or to visit a woman he had met there. To a man, they affirmed that their intent had been to return to the States. None had any pressing commitments at home to discourage them from going. Indeed, they often felt they could not extend the commitments of adulthood at home until they had returned from Australia. Sometimes the idea of travel and freedom, especially after the restraints of years of military service, had something to do with their reasons for going back. One was pushed to return by his sense of guilt and responsibility (he admitted that he delayed going back for his war bride for four years, but eventually returned for her, and stayed). Like the other sojourners, they were in transitional, or "crease," stages in their life cycles: old enough to be autonomous; uprooted by their military service; not yet committed to career, family, mortgage, or community; and perhaps feeling uncomfortable with a life back home. They often went with indefinite return plans because there was nothing to hold them, or pull them, back home. We estimate that about 11% fit this category.

Romance also plays a role as a self-instrumental motivating factor for some

Jews who moved to Israel. More American women than men migrate to Israel, and the desire to find a marital companion (although not limited to women) may be a motivating factor. Most of the persons we interviewed were married couples, and it is doubtful whether many of them would have confessed that they had come to find other persons even if that was their true motivation. However, almost all of the Americans who come to Israel to study (a self-instrumental motivation that is limited in time), whether in universities, teacher's institutes, or *yeshivot* (institutes of talmudic study), are single. Some of these persons do marry and remain in Israel. In some cases, the true motivating factor is the family of the student. Interviews with American parents of children in Israel occasionally elicited comments such as that made by one mother who said, "Thank God, Susan went to study in Israel and met a good Jewish boy. I don't mind at all helping them (financially). It is better than her remaining here single, or God forbid even worse, marrying someone who wasn't Jewish."

QUADRANT C OTHERS-EXPRESSIVE: FAMILY TIES

Early interviews in Australia revealed that many Yanks had decided to move there because of family commitments. They would not have even considered going and certainly not staying had it not been for their love and loyalty for kin who, for whatever reason, were tied to Australia. These Americans were motivated by a concern for the expressive needs of others.

Similarly, some Olim moved to Israel because of marriage to an Israeli who wished to return home or because of close connections with a branch of the family who went to Israel from a European, Asian, or African country while the other family branch went to the United States. Increasingly, some of these Olim are the American-born and/or -raised children of Israelis who left Israel for the United States. Participant observation in Israeli society uncovered these trends, but we lack the necessary data to quantify them.

We found that American women who married Australians often assumed that they would have to go there and stay for good. Bonner was one of these people who had lived in Australia since 1959, when she arrived with Steve, her recently married Australian husband. They had met in college in the States. As a result of their recent divorce, she now lived in a flat with two of their four children; the other two lived with Steve. Trained as a physical therapist, she was trying to set up her own office at the time of the interview and learning to become financially independent for the first time in her life. Her small apartment was hastily secured after the separation, and was far more modest than the house where she had lived for the last ten years. With no real family to return to in the States, and with no deep roots in Australia, Bonner felt she had to reevaluate her original decision to live in Australia the rest of her life. Now 37, she remained an American citizen:

I married an Australian when I was in school in the States, and I came here laboring under the illusion that it mattered very little where and under what circumstances one kept house. Of course, this led to a great many disillusions when I got here, but my stubbornness made me stay.

I think you'd practically go anywhere with someone you love. But the idea of making a new start did appeal to me. I was a little bit frightened of it. I was wondering what I'd find when I came here. I asked Australians a lot of questions when I left. I don't know if you've run into this characteristic of Australians, but they kid an awful lot, "rubbish" you. And most of the things they told me with absolute candor I just took as kidding, and found out to my horror when I arrived that they weren't. In fact, if anything, they were sort of understating some of the problems I'd strike.

Bonner's reasons for going as a settler illustrate the influence of family relationships, especially the intimate bond of marriage. It seemed reasonable to assume at the outset that settlers would more likely arrive in Australia with Australian spouses than would sojourners. Indeed, they were. About one third of the surveyed settlers, but only about one fifth of the sojourners, arrived married to Australians (31% and 18%, respectively).

Furthermore, nearly half of all settlers (49%) felt that their Australian-rooted family ties were important or very important in their decisions to migrate, compared with fewer than one third of the sojourners (30%). One out of three settlers felt that such ties were not important considerations, while more than half (54%) of the sojourners felt this way. Sojourners were often influenced by bonds of family in their decisions to spend some time in Australia: visiting parents, in-laws, children or perhaps just living there awhile near the Australian spouse's family. The marital relationship was probably the most important of these relationships, but the feelings of parents for their Australian-rooted children and of children for their Australia-bound parents were often decisive in settlement intentions. Overall, for 23% of the respondents marriage and family reunification figured in the motivations of respondents for migrating to Australia.

Bonner also resembled many other Yanks in the way she gathered information about Australia. She relied on Australians living in the States to provide her with all the information and assurances she needed to prepare for living there. Many Australians spoke highly of their country. Thus, Americans, with very limited sources of information about this somewhat romanticized land, became eager to learn more about this exotic place. The fact that Australians speak English assures Americans that it is, after all, another Anglo culture. (As we shall see later, they are generally correct.) Settlers and sojourners alike said they learned more from Australians or other Yanks who had lived there than from all other possible sources of information. Moving to Australia was not usually seen as a permanent relocation, fraught with unknown consequences and traumas. Rather, it was generally thought of as a temporary move, posing few risks and therefore requiring little information to prepare for the move.

Bonner's circumstances reflect the typical situation of most Americans, settlers and sojourners alike. She, too, was in a transitional stage in her life when she moved to Australia: a college student without a job and a newly married woman just leaving her home. Going to Australia would not uproot her from integration into community, career, or family. It would, in fact, help to solidify her integration into her own nuclear family. Besides, moving abroad promised to be an exciting adventure.

Many interviews revealed a wide variety of family relationships that took Americans to Australia. We interviewed Ed, a settler whose Australian wife's desire to return to her family was decisive in his decision to move to Australia for good; they sold their house and car, bade farewell to friends and professional colleagues, and left. But in his case, economic and personal considerations were involved as well as family loyalty. Ed was an alcoholic and very uneasy with the life-style of Hollywood, where he worked as an entertainer (see quadrant A, Ed and Cass). Terry was an American ex-serviceman who decided to retire there because his children (by his Australian wife) and his mother-in-law all lived there. He was settled with his wife, her sister, and a niece. One American named Stanley explained that he was brought to Australia by migrating (retiring military) parents 16 years earlier. Daphne was brought by her parents when she was 17, along with four brothers and sisters. Both Chris and Susan married Australia-bound Englishmen, knowing it meant a permanent stay. Overall, 37% of the settler survey respondents agreed that they arrived intending to stay in large part because of family circumstances.

Family concerns were also important for many sojourners. While not quite as likely as settlers to consider Australian family ties important in their reasons for moving there, nonetheless nearly one sojourner in three said this was a significant consideration. Overall, 23% of the sojourner males arrived with Australian spouses, as did 11% of the female sojourners. Moreover, American servicemen had stronger Australian family ties than others: of the 55 surveyed Americans who had been to Australia earlier with the military, 66% had returned with Australian wives. This compares with 36% of all respondents, 26% of all males, and 16% of all surveyed females.

There were several routes by which Australian family commitments grew into decisions to migrate. Usually the spouse's longing for family was coupled with the Yank's weaker family integration. So why not spend a year or two in Australia? The cultural expectation that wives would go where husbands went also drew many Americans. Australian husbands were drawn back not only by family yearnings, but also by pragmatic concerns for finding work. But their wives were concerned with preserving the strength of the family bond. Either way, Yanks were migrating to meet the needs of their Australian spouses, who usually wanted to return for expressive reasons: they wanted to go back home.

The desire to "go back home," which we have seen affects the decision of some native American Jews to move to Israel, also has an others-expressive impact in the Israeli case. Among the interviews we conducted with Americans living in Israel, we found that in one of five cases one spouse said the motivation to come was to remain together as a family; and that it was the other spouse who wanted to move. In this case, it was always a woman who made such a statement. Twenty-one percent of the 107 persons who responded to a questionnaire in the United States addressed to parents of Americans in Israel (Parents of North American Israelis Study) said that their child had moved in order to be with a spouse, rather than because of the child's own belief that the move was a good one. The spouse in almost all of these cases as well was the woman. While this latter group did include a few American women married to Israeli men, in most of the cases both partners in marriage were Americans.

QUADRANT D OTHERS-INSTRUMENTAL: SERVICE PERSONNEL

Historically, a substantial number of pioneers in Palestine (before Israel attained statehood) were primarily interested in forming a new type of society, one in which the Jews would constitute the majority population and move from a position of second-class citizenship in the "old" country to one of dominance. The idea was to forge an independent and self-sufficient society. This demanded a willingness to contribute to the collective and to put into abeyance one's own desires and needs. Indeed, in some kibbutzim, or collective settlements, marriages had been forbidden because the personal, almost egoistic, wishes of the couple to be together could be seen as threatening the communal nature of the general body. Such a "selfish" act as wishing to raise children would clearly lead to a decrease in the number of able bodies capable of working the land, plowing the fields, and building roads. For a time, then, even having children was frowned upon in some elements, since it meant that "productive" workers would be removed from the work force. The point of all this is to demonstrate the others-instrumental orientation that characterized these people. They had a concrete goal in mind and it was externally oriented to the benefit of others, even if it meant foregoing their own personal wishes and desires.

Much of the early mass migration to post-state Israel was composed of the ingathering of the exiles, the rescue of refugees who had no other place to which to turn as they fled a ravaged Europe or sought to escape persecution in Arab countries. It is basically irrelevant to discuss their motivation for migration—it was, quite simply, a question of survival. Still, others-instrumental-oriented pioneers kept coming. American immigrants to Israel who wish to feel that they are making a contribution to the society in which they live are among this group. To some extent, this is the obverse side of the self-expressive coin. Personal satisfaction is manifested in a self-expressive motivation. This means that one migrates for personal, almost existential, happiness. By contrast, individuals in the others-instrumental category obtained satisfaction by knowing that they are doing something useful and constructive for others who are important to them. Wishing to live a life in a majority Jewish environment includes the hope that they can make a positive contribution to their adopted land. Their motto, to use President John F. Kennedy's words, is "ask not what your country can do for you, but what you can do for your country."

Zev, a former businessman, came to Israel and started growing organic fruits and vegetables, and plants and flowers. His new work kept him and his wife busy seven days a week from early morning until late at night. He readily admits that he is in constant financial difficulties since he came, "but the good Lord keeps the banks after me all the time so that, thank God, I don't even have time to sit down and worry about what trouble I'm in." Is he sorry that he came?

> You have to be kidding! I came to work this land and help build this country. I have absolutely nothing to complain about. If there is any complaint I have, it's that I didn't come sooner, and that more people don't come. If we all pitch in and do what we can, we can make this country really something.

Others-instrumental motivation can characterize a different type of migrant as well. The missionary who has to move elsewhere in order to seek potential converts is also manifesting an others-instrumental motivation. The difference is that the specific choice of location for such a person is not geographically determined, but rather is cultural. The missionary can preach in many different areas, wherever potential believers can be found. The medical personnel on a Project Hope ship can assist others in need in a variety of countries, always moving on when a project is completed or when a greater emergency arises elsewhere. Indeed, if the suitable needy can be found at home, the preacher and doctor need not move at all. The others-instrumental migrant to Israel, however, has no choice. It is because of the feeling that Israel is *the* Jewish state that working for others there takes on a special significance. Teaching in a Jewish school or working in a Jewish hospital in the United States is not a satisfactory substitute for these people.

Izzy is an ophthalmic surgeon who gave up a million-dollar practice to work in a hospital in Israel (and to find himself part of a nationwide doctors' strike soon after he moved there in protest of the meager wages paid government physicians):

> I came because when I treat somebody here, I'm treating family. I mean it really makes a difference to me that these people are mine and that I identify with them. I've had many more interesting cases back in the States, and there's nothing to talk about as far as money goes, but it wasn't the person I cared about there but the case. Here I'm helping a man or woman or child who I really care about because together we make up this place. Maybe I sound racist, but it's really a form of patriotism and no different back in the States for many people there. That song—"he's not heavy, he's my brother"—I thought it was great, but I personally never felt it. I know that some of my colleagues did, and especially in the military. Here it's true all the time . . . I'm not

saying that it's important for everybody to feel something personal about the work
they do. But considering the way I was brought up in Jewish schools and Zionist youth
movements, it was almost natural that I should feel this way.

A particularly interesting group of individuals with others-instrumental motives are rabbis belonging to the Conservative and Reform denominations. The
dominant stream of Judaism in Israel is Orthodoxy, even though the majority of
Israel's Jews are not religiously observant. Some Reform, and especially Conservative clergy, have moved to Israel in order to introduce their more liberal
religious movements to a country that they feel needs a religious revival and a
movement that is more adapted to the religious needs of modern, contemporary
society.

While these rabbis are moving away from the United States to help Judaism
develop elsewhere, they differ from the classic missionary in that they would not
have moved to just any country that was in need of a Jewish revival. Nor would
they have moved to Israel to merely feel that they were fulfilling a religious
commandment or satisfying a personal, religious desire. What differentiates the
instrumental others from the expressive self-motivation is that the latter *is* satisfied by just being there. Knowing that one is in Israel is, for some, enough to
satisfy their identity needs. For the others-instrumental-motivated migrant, however, it is more than that. It is an active feeling of doing something for "significant others" that is truly important. For some—teachers, farmers, doctors, and
even rabbis—these "significant others" are only located in a tiny strip along the
Mediterranean Sea and it is to that location that they move.[1]

THE VIEWS OF THOSE LEFT BEHIND

Some more insight on the motivations for migration can be gained by
examining the responses of those left behind—the parents of emigrants. Such an
opportunity exists with regard to a sample of the parents of American Israelis,
who belonged to an association of such parents.

In 1974, some of the parents of Americans who had moved to Israel formed
an organization called the Association of Parents of American Israelis (APAI).
Today the group calls itself PNAI (Parents of North American Israelis). In recent

[1]From the discussion in this section it emerges that quadrant D (others-instrumental) often incorpo-
rates an element of self-expressive consideration in that aid rendered unto others provides a feeling
of self-satisfaction in and of itself. The success of the intervention is not even crucial. While the
measure of success for purely instrumental considerations is whether the goal was indeed achieved,
there is a degree of satisfaction with regard to the others-instrumental quadrant in knowing that an
effort was made. Missionaries whose attempts to "save" souls may be unsuccessful and physicians
whose patients do not fully recover may, nevertheless, derive satisfaction from knowing that they
themselves did the best they could.

years, the membership of this association has reached over 2,000 families. This association has organized chapters in the larger Jewish communities of the United States and Canada with periodic meetings to discuss Israeli issues and, in particular, the issues facing them and their children. The association also publishes a national newsletter.

The data reported here were collected on the occasion of the tenth anniversary convention held in Israel in 1984. During this convention the association gathered data on its members using a questionnaire filled in by those parents who attended the convention. The information thus gathered provided valuable insight into how very close relatives view one group of American emigrants. Despite the fact that these data do not derive from a representative sample of such parents, they do yield insights not generally available about the experience of leaving a country from those left behind.

One of the questions in the survey asked, "What do you see as (PNAI's) role in your life?" The most frequent reply (55%) was that (PNAI) is "a support group." The following replies demonstrates this: "This was my lifeline. To make me feel that I'm not the only parent whose child left for such a far away land." Or, "it creates the feeling of an extended family. It is important to me as a support group, as a medium to help parents who have a real problem adjusting to their child's desertion." Finally, "PNAI gives me solace to meet with others who empathize with me." There is no difference in the percentage of people who see PNAI as a support group among those parents who hold a positive, a negative, or a neutral attitude toward the decision of their children to move to Israel. Just about all of these parents who responded said that their children had made one or more visits to Israel, which in 36% of the cases had been for a year or longer. They gave a variety of reasons as to why their children decided to move to Israel. Fourteen percent of these parents said that the quite positive experiences in Israel of their children strongly motivated them to migrate. Yet, 21% felt that the main motivation of their own child was the very strong desire of their child's spouse to live in Israel.

These parents did not view visits to Israel as equivalent to visiting some other place, say, European countries. Rather, visits by their children to Israel were viewed as somewhat risky in that such an event can start off a chain reaction that results in their children moving to Israel. Even before their child's first visit to Israel, these parents, and probably others like them, were afraid of such visits and the resultant influence on their child. Parents did not attribute their children's motivations to a desire to get away from the United States, but rather to a positive wish to live in Israel. Nine percent said the motivations stemmed from their Zionist home or background; 6% said their children wished to make a contribution to the Jewish state; 12% said that the children wished to live as Jews in Israel; and 5% said that their children simply always had wanted to go there.

For some, the desire to live life as a Jew in Israel seemed to be related to a decision to adopt Orthodox Judaism. Several of the parents explained that their children had decided to start observing the traditional precepts of Judaism. They then felt that this could best be done in Israel.

Eight percent of the parents said their children were looking for "meaning in life"; 3% said they felt that in Israel the children would be able to fulfill their pioneering spirit; 1% felt they were looking for adventure; and 2% stated that their children said it would be better to bring up their own offspring in Israel.

Finally, many parents were not really sure why their children decided to migrate. Even though they said their children were Zionists, they still asked themselves why it was *their* children who actually made the move. This was dramatically stated by one parent who, in an interview at the 1984 conference, quite seriously said that he just did not understand it. He had sent his son to Jewish schools, Jewish summer camps, and programs in Israel. So where did he go wrong, he asked, that his son later decided to leave his parents and move to Israel?

Parents were asked their reactions to their children's initial decision to move to Israel. Nineteen percent of the respondents expressed support and pride, with no negative feelings added. Statements made by some include "I'm thrilled. He's living my dream." "He had our complete blessings." "I thought it was terrific." "I was supportive."

The reaction of 18% of the parents related to the independence of their children. Said one, "it's her life and I have to respect her decision." One parent rhetorically asked whether any parent has the right to tell a child what he or she can do.

Such reactions, though, were not the norm. In general, respondents' reactions were mixed. Thirty percent of the parents said their reactions were both positive and negative, with two variations on this theme. One variation was that they were proud of their children although the decision to leave was personally sad to them. The other variation was that they were happy for their children in having made a decision that was important to them although they, themselves, felt lonely and sad.

Thirty-one percent of the parents expressed only a negative reaction, and this was more marked among parents of girls than parents of boys. Some of the parents merely stated what their own personal feelings were: "Heartbreak"; "Upset, despair, anger"; "Shock and displeasure." Others explained that their feelings were based upon the difficulty of living in an economically and politically troubled country such as Israel. "Why would you want to live there? 'It's hard financially,' I said, and I was proven right." Others said that they "fear for their safety," or that they are "disappointed because it is so far away and a poor country and politically insecure." Several referred to the fact that they would have preferred their children to complete their education in the United States. "I was unhappy because he didn't finish college, and it is a waste of his mind to live on a kibbutz. He was always an overachiever and now he is only following instructions."

SUMMARY

Americans who have migrated to Australia and Israel have been impelled by diverse goals, motives, and circumstances. No simple "push-pull" analysis is adequate to explain their decisions. There are some common background features that help to explain not why they went, but why they were able to go. Many of these Americans were at crossroads in their life cycles that typically dislodge people from bonds to parents, extended family, and community. The search for work was especially important: Many were beginning their careers, had completed their formal training (usually college), and had few commitments to employer or locale to restrain them. Instilled with the American values of travel, independence, and adventure, they were easily enticed by an opportunity to live abroad—but not necessarily for good. Although they were no longer tied to family back home, they often went as nuclear family units. So, social integration was important to them, defined as commitment to spouses and children rather than to parents. Their educational background assured them of secure employment in Australia and Israel, as well as America if they ever decided to return. That is, they did not feel that they were taking a risk. Without an intention to settle permanently, they did not have to bid farewell to family, friends, and country.

Many Americans moved to Australia and Israel with the intention of staying. But their motives are not easily explained by the push-pull metaphors. Few complained of dire economic straits back in America, although career crises had an effect on a few. Personal alienation was an important factor for many, especially those who went to Israel. The need to resolve religioethnic identities, however, was a very different type of alienation than the more secular social estrangement that a few Yanks in Australia described. Furthermore, the settlers in Australia as well as Israel were more likely to migrate to maintain personal relationships than to escape oppressive social environments. Estrangement played a part in American emigration abroad, but family loyalty was more important. Simple explanations are not sufficient. Indeed, our typology, based on the four quadrants, suggests the complexity of migration motives as well as the responses and reactions of those left behind, in this case, the parents of American emigrants to Israel.

Thus, most Americans go to Israel to fulfill personal, social, and/or religious ideals and to resolve their Jewish identities (a self-expressive motivation). In contrast, Americans usually go to Australia to work temporarily (self-instrumental), to maintain or strengthen their immediate family group (others-expressive), to experience a taste of adventure (self-expressive), or to escape an alienating environment or experience (again, self-expressive). The expressive column implies spiritual, emotional, or value fulfillment; instrumental implies material or task achievement.

Having said this, we do note that those bound for Israel and Australia are traveling to a land that, while foreign, is not *too* foreign. The preconceived notion of a fundamental cultural similarity means that the immigrants are headed toward a country that falls within what might be called a latitude of identity that is acceptably close to that which initially characterizes the migrant. Enough adaptation (or adjustment) is required to provide such migrants with the feeling that they are making a change, and even to take pride in their cultural flexibility and more universal orientation than those who remain behind. However, there is also a feeling that the amount of change required is limited to a level that will not overtax the senses and entail an unbearable burden. For such migrants, the change is conceptually quantitative rather than qualitative—more or less of the same, but not something fundamentally different.

It is much easier to explain why these people actually stayed in Israel and Australia than why they went there in the first place. Decisions to stay or leave were often linked to original settlement intentions. But for many, especially Yanks in Australia, permanent settlement seemed to happen to them, without any real decisions being made. Difficult adjustments to and unrealistic expectations of the new society could lead to disillusionment. Settlers knew it would probably be tough to start over, and were usually prepared to face these difficulties. For many, the ease of adjustments, especially in Australia, led to continual deferral of their plans to return. We turn now to examining in detail the question of how the emigrants adapted to their adopted societies.

5

Adjustments

How They Adapt

In a recent interview, one of the most well-known American emigrants of the movie world, Stanley Kubrick, mused about his experiences living abroad in England:

> If you live, say, in New York, you get the images of your neighborhood and your friends, but essentially it's all the electronic-village stuff, and it isn't that different now living anyplace, with cities being decentralized and computer modems and TV. (Grove, 1987, p. 65)

Kubrick is suggesting that rapid means of communication and transportation have reduced the physical and emotional distance of living abroad, and made it easier to adjust in a new environment. This chapter explains just how easy or hard these adjustments are and the variety of challenges the emigrants faced.

In moving abroad, most migrants arrive with some initial impressions about their new country. Indeed, one of the difficulties in adjustment relates to the impressions they bring with them as well as their conceptions of the way life ought to be organized there.

These impressions are based on views derived from their home society. Whether these impressions and views are accurate or not may affect the degree of ease or difficulty in adjusting to the new society.

Once individuals decide to emigrate and actually do so, the subsequent absorption process they experience affects their ultimate decision to remain in their adopted land or return to their home country. The adjustments that we describe in this chapter provide the background for understanding the succeeding chapters which provide an explanation as to why the emigrants remain or return. The variety of adjustments the emigrants experience represent the "tempest-tossed seas" on which are played out the drama of whether to stay on the newfound shore or return to the one left behind.

73

ADJUSTMENT IN AUSTRALIA

Doubtless, Americans face more potential problems when they move abroad than when relocating to another part of the States. However, in moving to Australia, they generally expected to face few adjustment problems, and it is no wonder they felt this way. Even the most naive of them who knew virtually nothing about Australia often decided to move there simply because it is an English-speaking country. The freedom to converse without having to learn a new language was extremely important. Furthermore, use of English also implied that the basic Anglo-European culture would be familiar: values, history, traditions, food, beliefs, music, literature, styles and standards of living, consumer products, and so on. Hopefully, the institutions would be similar as well: hospitals, schools, professions, stores, and so forth. The first impressions of Australia as the Boeing 747 approaches Melbourne provide an American who knows Southern California with familiar sights: the sprawling suburbs, the red-tiled ranch-style houses, and streets choked with traffic. Many Americans commented upon arrival that: "it's just like America," or "just like America used to be." It is, in fact, a foreign country. The unknowing Yank could be forgiven for not noticing the differences right away.

Many Yanks had already removed much of the guesswork about Australia through previous visits (vacations, military service) or social contacts with Australians (spouses, friends) and other Americans (usually someone who had been there during World War II or on "R and R" during the Vietnam War, or a returning tourist). Any American who had never visited Australia could easily sense that he or she would find it familiar simply by knowing an Australian or two in the States. Australians seem comfortable in the United States. They adapt easily. They converse fluently with a distinct but understandable accent. They joke with a recognizable sense of humor. One of the authors, for example, met his first Australian at 15, the mother of a friend. Aside from her charming accent, she was by no means foreign or alien. She and other Australians clearly found Americans and America quite familiar. Just knowing one Australian could convince a naive American that a stay in Australia would be quite manageable without too much strain.

The uncertain migrant often researched the country, scouring libraries for books and magazines, digesting the consulate-supplied literature, watching the rare television or movie documentary, or even a feature film with Australia as the background. National Geographic magazine articles about Australia could convince someone that Australia was a distinctly familiar place. The cities, the suburbs, the cars, all were strikingly familiar. Certainly the unique character of Australia is highly publicized: Alice Springs, the Outback, the cave-dwelling opal miners of Coober Pedy, the aborigines, and the koalas and kangaroos. But behind the exotica, the general impression is that Australia is an Anglo country, with a way of life Americans might find quaint but not really alien. The media tended to exaggerate the similarities between Australia and America and minimized potential differences; or they romanticized Australia in images of the Outback or the Last Frontier—certainly images that Australians find appealing, but no more accurate than characterizing America as a land of cowboys. (In fact, 4 out of 5 Australians live in the coast-hugging cities. Melbourne had about 3 million and Sydney had $3\frac{1}{4}$ million people in 1980.) Consequently, Americans merely informed by the media probably were not as well prepared as other Americans with a wider source of information.

While most Americans went to Australia believing there would be few significant problems of adjustment, nevertheless, they expected some inconveniences or frustrations. Even the Yanks returning to Australia knew they would have to cope with a new way of life. Those who had been "fooled" into believing Australia was "just like America" were usually surprised and often disappointed to learn otherwise. First appearances, they would explain, were deceiving, and by their second year, they had finally begun to discover the "real Australia." But by and large, Americans learned to cope with the new way of life and often lost much of their self-consciousness as foreigners. They stopped feeling like aliens and started feeling as though they fit in. Not that they actually believed they were "really Australians," of course. Reminders that they were "really Americans" were frequent enough through daily social discourse, with people politely asking, "Are you American or Canadian?" ("Canadian," because Australians had learned that Canadians cherished their national identity and did not like to be mistaken for Americans.) With a little effort, they could fit in so well that they often found they were leading "normal" lives.

Yanks who needed reassurance that they shared a remarkably similar culture with Australians had only to look around at other recently arrived non-English-speaking immigrants. Australia's cities teemed with hundreds of thousands of newcomers whose dress and physical features indicated that they were obviously very different from Australians. Their ethnic newspapers were visible at news stands. Their restaurants and shops were evident throughout the city. Large numbers of immigrants worked in the milk bars (somewhat like convenience stores in the States) and fish-and-chips carryouts. Their neighborhoods and communities had become socially distinct (and often consisted of high-rise public housing complexes, something very few Australians ever experienced). Yanks were well aware that these people had it much tougher than they did finding work, making friends, and fitting in. In its 1969 Survey of American Settlers, the Australian Department of Labour and Immigration noted:

> This evidence (showing their success at finding suitable employment) is in keeping with the general similarity which exists in the Australian economy when compared with that of the United States. This similarity means that American settlers are much less likely to be subject to major disruptions in their employment patterns on emigra-

tion and settlement in Australia than is quite often the case for migrants from other origins, particularly Southern and Eastern Europe. (p. 30)

It did not take Americans long to discover that many Australians disliked these new, non-Anglo newcomers—and that Americans were definitely not in that group. The Americans we interviewed realized that they enjoyed a privileged status. They generally had arrived with high educational and professional qualifications, often with well-paid jobs awaiting them or relatively easy to find. Unlike the other, much poorer immigrants, Americans usually arrived with adequate bankrolls to draw from, including enough money to pay their way back. All things considered, Americans had little to complain about, and they knew it. As Bardo and Bardo (1980c) point out, Yanks shared a norm of not expressing a complaint. We found this to be true as well, so much so that many were reluctant to "rubbish" features about Australia that they found dissatisfying or very different from back in the States. Australians, they quickly learned, did not appreciate hearing about their faults or America's supposed superiority, and tended to disparage such complainers as "whingers."

Most Yanks (80%) could recall something that had caused exasperation, anger, confusion, or bewilderment and that required a significant adjustment. Some were extremely bothered by the unending chill of winter (as most did not have central heating) while others hated the giant Huntsman spiders.

The wages were generally lower and the taxes were higher. Durable goods like automobiles and appliances were much more costly; many items were in short supply or had only recently become available. Urban land and housing were generally more expensive than in America, rental accommodations were relatively scarce, and housing usually lacked such amenities as central heating and indoor toilets. Items common in America were often not available in stores, and shopping hours were more restricted than in America. Many complained about adjusting to driving on the left side of the road (and steering wheels in Australian cars are positioned on the right side); the road conditions were poor, and Australian driving habits seemed reckless and aggressive. Americans had to adjust to the metric system, and American children had to adjust to a very different school system.

One author's early adjustment, and one that most Yanks found annoying, was coping with frequent strikes in this heavily unionized society, in this case by baggage handlers at the airports. Later, a postal strike threatened to abort the distribution of the survey for this research. In fact, while the data were being gathered, there were also nationwide strikes of airline pilots, truck drivers, and garbage haulers. We talked with several Americans who were exasperated with the political power of the unions and the politics of a parliamentary democracy. Many were sensitive to a growing anti-American sentiment. ("Yankee go home" slogans were spray-painted on buildings near Melbourne University.) As with any place, the climate irritated some. And being accustomed to diversity, a few found the overwhelming Anglo-uniformity of Australia too boring and bland, while a few others preferred it to living in a multiracial society. As similar as it seemed, there were differences, and sometimes Yanks found them very irritating indeed.

Still, all found ways to cope with such things gradually. They took them in stride, eventually took them for granted, and finally bragged about them on return visits to the States. But these were not the most serious problems Americans faced. The toughest adjustments were rooted in fundamental, and often very subtle, differences between the two cultures.

It is interesting how it sometimes took Americans six months to a year to discover just how different they were from the Australians. The Australians placed a lower value on material consumption, and the general pace of life was more relaxed and leisurely than in the States. In particular, Australians preferred an unhurried work ethic ("she'll be right" was the general term for it). American women were often discouraged by the prevailing masculine (some might say antifemale) culture. Finally, we found that for most Americans, adjusting to Australia can be a lifelong process. However, such adjustments did not often provoke alienation from Australian life. For the Yanks were right: Australia is so much like America that, adjustments notwithstanding, Americans have an easy time fitting into it.

ADJUSTMENT IN ISRAEL

As noted in Chapter 2, the Israeli census of 1983 reported there were 37,327 U.S.-born persons living in Israel. This is quite a sizable jump in the number of U.S.-born in Israel from 3,550 reported in the 1961 census. Indeed, the number of American settlers in Israel in 1983 is very similar to those in Australia at about the same time (32,620 in 1982). The growing volume of migrants in the late 1960s and 1970s (as noted in Chapter 2) undoubtedly made it easier for succeeding waves of Americans to adjust to their new surroundings through the beginning of an Anglo-ethnic subgroup composed of all English-speaking immigrants. Also, Israeli living standards rose at the same time.

If Americans moving to Australia expected to find a quaint Americanized Anglo-society, Americans moving to Israel expected to find an authentic, normal, indigenous Jewish culture. This is impressed on the first-time American visitor to Israel traveling on El Al Israel Airlines. As the plane begins its descent to Tel Aviv, the public address system plays a joyful rendition of *hevenu shalom aleikhem*, a traditional Hebrew song of greeting, and a pop hit, *am yisrael hai* (the Jewish people lives).

Of course, there were obvious differences between American, Jewish, and Israeli cultures: Israeli manners, which tend to be more casual; the more lackadaisical approach to worker productivity and business efficiency; and even the food, which is more Middle Eastern and spicy in taste than American Jewish cuisine, which is predominately of Eastern European origins.

An organizational sociologist, Benjamin Phillips, who had worked for General Motors in the United States before moving to Israel, lists Israel among those countries most lacking long-range planning and, instead, making do by continuous improvisations (Danon, 1988). This is something that quite bothers American migrants.

Time in Israel seems to stand still. Shmuel, a 47-year-old free-lance translator, rationalizes this by explaining that "in a country with a 2,000-year history, what does the average clerk care if you don't get what you want today when they tell you to come tomorrow? For him, that must seem like immediate service." It is no wonder that one of the first street-wise words that Americans in Israel quickly pick up is *savlanut* (patience). The second one is *shvita* (strike) because part of the reason for the need for *savlanut* is that many institutions controlled by the public sector (schools, hospitals, sanitation workers, postal services, etc.) seem to be on strike much more often than in the United States. One American complained that when there is a "work to rule" mail strike, it takes a whole week for a letter to be delivered within the same city, but when there is no strike it only takes seven days!

The slower pace of life is manifested even in store hours. Many stores close one afternoon during midweek, in addition to following the Mediterranean custom of closing for an afternoon siesta on a regular basis. A popular Israeli joke is that the government wants to institute a five-day workweek (instead of the current six), but they will do it gradually. First they will get people used to working one day a week, and then to two days, and so on.

Manners and orientations regarding time are all obvious differences that require getting used to. One of the main problems of a new immigrant in Israel is that in a bureaucratized country the immigrant has to take care of dozens of government-related matters within a short time. The same number of government contacts would normally be spread over years for a native resident. The immigrant has to acquire his or her Israeli driver's license, join a medical welfare fund, buy or rent an apartment, arrange for electricity, gas, and water services, register children for school (and spend extra time with them helping them get over their own acculturation difficulties), look for a job, and all of this while waiting for a telephone. (At the time of this study it often took several months to get a telephone. The phone and postal systems have since been reorganized, considerably improving service in both areas.)

At first blush, the bureaucracy can seem overwhelming. Various government and nongovernment agencies are responsible for different aspects of absorption rights and privileges, thus assuring that immigrants will be kept running to different offices. Thus, government benefits designed to assist immigrants ironically contribute to the feelings of frustration with bureaucracy. Amiel, a young immigrant who was kept busy at the bank changing dollars into Israeli currency to finance his recently purchased apartment, could not get over a system that requires that the bank clerk take up everyone's time by filling out the forms himself. He particularly "enjoyed" watching the clerk always tear up the third copy of a four-copy form because it was not needed. That never stopped the clerk from fastidiously making sure the carbon paper was in place for the third copy.

Shlomit, an astute American immigrant who had obviously studied sociology, complained about the way that information is so closely guarded in order to retain power:

> It's clear that if they publish the information, let's say about what you are entitled to, then you won't need the clerk to tell it to you. So he has to guard his position and make sure it doesn't get published. But you don't even know what to ask him, since you don't know what is available, so then it all comes down to your personal relationship with the clerk. If you get him to like you, he'll tell you what you need to know, and not just react to what you specifically ask.

This brings us to the way that Israelis, in general, get along in their bureaucratized society. The method of adaptation is called *proteksia*, or "pull." The trick is to know someone who can pull strings to have your affairs handled speedily. One American who wanted some personal attention in the dermatology department of a large hospital asked her neighbor, whose sister-in-law had a cousin who is a nurse in the orthopedics department at the same hospital, to make the necessary contact in the dermatology department.

While everyone complains about *proteksia*, the best way of fighting it is to adapt to it, and Americans do an admirable job at that (Danet and Hartman, 1972). Naomi, a homemaker who recently built a house outside of Jerusalem, gives an example of this:

> We had to get so many forms signed and permission from so many government offices that we would never have finished it without the assistance of Yitzhak, a neighbor of ours. He knows everybody and a phone call from him always led people to be more helpful to us. There was nothing in it for him, or for them. They didn't owe anything to Yitzhak, it's just sort of an old boy network. So why did he help us? I think that he likes having an American as a friend.

Another reason, perhaps, is that some Israelis like to show others that they can arrange things.

Let us look at the data on satisfaction with aspects of life in Israel. After one year, 46% of the U.S. migrants who worked outside the home reported that they were very much satisfied with their work situation in contrast to just 26% among all other migrants. After one year in Israel, 27% of the U.S. migrants and 25% of all other migrants were very much satisfied with their social life. U.S. migrants were more inclined to seek out migrants from other countries. After one year, 24% of them reported that they often engaged in social activities with migrants from other countries in contrast to just 18% for such other migrants.

On the other hand, U.S. migrants were less inclined to socialize with "long-time" U.S. migrants than were other migrants with their own veteran settlers. After one year in Israel, 28% of the U.S. migrants reported often sharing social activities with veteran U.S. migrants in contrast to 32% of all other migrants. However, after one year in Israel, 44% of U.S. migrants reported socializing often with Israelis or other veteran migrants (from countries other than the United States) in contrast to 26% of all other migrants. Nevertheless, U.S. migrants were considerably less sure of staying in Israel than were all other migrants. After one year, just 36% of them were certain they would stay and 18% were pretty certain, while among all other migrants 67% were certain they would stay and 18% were pretty certain of this.

After two months in Israel, U.S. migrants showed a slight lead with regard to knowledge of Hebrew. Among them, 28% claimed they could speak Hebrew freely in contrast to 15% of all other migrants; 42% of the U.S. migrants and 42% of all other migrants could speak Hebrew, but with difficulty. Finally, just 30% of the U.S. migrants but 43% of all other migrants could not speak Hebrew at all. The ability to learn the language is related to age. An elderly American neighbor of one of the authors would make two trips to the local grocery store to buy a dozen eggs because she never learned how to count past 6 in Hebrew and was too embarrassed to try to make herself understood by sign language. She never did overcome the metric system. Instead, she preferred asking visiting friends to bring in clothing items in American sizes that she needed and even "imported" thermometers so that she did not have to read temperatures in centigrade.

Currently at least a quarter of all Americans in Israel do return to the United States, and so these conditions cannot be downplayed. However, what actually needs explaining is why so many Americans do remain. In this connection we note that the primary motivation for their original emigration was related to their "expressive" needs. This is the essential point. To overcome the difficulties of Israeli life, various pamphlets have been published by veteran immigrants ("Things My Immigration Emissary Never Told Me" is one of them), but perhaps most telling is the fact that there is a 600-page book published by the North American Aliyah Movement (which is the American-based organization that is a counterpart to the Association of Americans and Canadians in Israel). This book is designed to help immigrants deal with the concrete problems of moving and getting settled in Israel and is entitled *Coming Home*.

There is one other important fact that should be mentioned. As in Australia, other immigrants to Israel are looked down on as newcomers, while Americans (and everything American) enjoy relatively high prestige. A standard advertising ploy in Israel is to brag about the "American quality" of the Israeli-made product or to play up the fact that a particular product is American-made. The country that is the most popular tourist site for those Israelis who can afford it is the United States. (It is also the most popular destination for Israeli emigrants.)

Americans come with a high degree of education and feel that they know more than the "backward natives." They feel that the U.S. political system is better and more democratic than the Israeli parliamentary system. In short, the label of new immigrant does not carry a negative connotation to the same degree as it does for immigrants from some other countries, such as the Eastern European bloc countries. Other immigrants will speak quietly when using their mother tongue in public, and even switch to Hebrew when passing by Israeli strangers. Americans freely speak out loudly in English and expect everyone to understand them. In fact, Israelis *are* all too pleased to speak English with American immigrants and to admire them for coming, even as they fail to understand why anyone would leave the land of Dallas and Dynasty with all the riches and opportunities that all Americans there must surely enjoy.

In sum, the U.S. migrants we studied adjusted fairly rapidly to the requirements of daily life in Israel. They were satisfied with their jobs, their social life was enjoyable, they had developed contacts with native-born Israelis and they were acquiring an adequate command of Hebrew. Yet, after a year in the country, they were still much less certain that they would stay than were other migrants. After all, leaving Israel is almost as easy, if not easier, than coming to Israel. The United States was but half a day's flying time away, and they had both an American passport and the money required to buy a return ticket.

CHALLENGES TO ADJUSTMENT IN FOUR QUADRANTS

Emigration is an experience fraught with challenges to be overcome. For most emigrants throughout human history, there probably was no possibility of turning back; for return meant servitude or subservience, oppression or suppression, despair or death. However, in the case of American emigrants, there is an option to return to the United States. Hence, an assessment of the challenges to adjustment ought to take this into account.

How can such adjustment challenges in Australia and Israel be organized, analyzed, and understood? We seek to do this in Table 5.1 by considering the two dimensions about which such challenges emerge. (See Chapter 3 for a similar analysis of migration motivation.) First is the axis of the "locus of concern," which is oriented either about the "self" or "others," such as family members. The other axis is the "adjustment challenge," which is centered about "expressive" dimensions of life, such as children's education or family satisfaction, or around "instrumental" areas of life, such as job, housing, and the like. Table 5.1

Table 5.1. Challenge of Adjustment

Locus of concern	Adjustment challenge	
	Expressive	Instrumental

Self	Way of life
	Sense of community and
	  belonging
	Host "personality"
	
	A
		Work
		Housing
		Daily standard of
		  living
		
		B

	C	D

Others	Children's education
	Family unity and
	  solidarity
		Medical service
		Medical care for
		  family
		Corporate transfer

illustrates the variety of challenges that may beset emigrants in the four quadrants. Thus, in quadrant A the challenge is to expressive activities revolving about the self and in quadrant B it is to instrumental activities about the self. In quadrant C the challenge is based on expressive activities centered about others and in quadrant D it is on instrumental activities focused also about service to others.

In Chapter 3 we presented a similar analysis of motivations for migration and we found that such motivations were clustered in quadrant A or self-expressive. Nevertheless, the factors that lead to a migration decision are not the same as the ones that produce adjustment in the new society. The instrumental concerns of quadrants B and D are likely to take initial precedence over the expressive concerns in quadrants A and C. One must reestablish a daily routine of living for oneself and one's family (if there is a family). Housing has to be acquired, work obtained, a new bureaucracy encountered and accommodated, and so forth. If a serious breakdown occurs in any of these vital areas for oneself or members of one's family, the adjustment process will fall apart. If this happens, the type of migrant with which we deal will return to the United States.

After adequate adjustments to quadrant B (and to a much lesser extent quadrant D), the instrumental factors, the migrants then focus upon the expressive factors of quadrants A and C. One seeks friends, education, satisfaction for self and family, the ability to handle a new language, as in Israel, or a new variation of one's native tongue as in Australia. Just as there is an initial focus on quadrant B self-instrumental concerns in adjustment and subsequent transition to other quadrants, so we might anticipate that this one quadrant may not be sufficient to explain whether the emigrants remain in the host country or return home, a subject to be examined later in this book. Gradually, almost without being aware of it, those migrants who get this far in the adjustment process acquire increasing amounts of emotional pleasure and satisfaction from their new situation. The emotional identification with the new society grows and grows. One is more and more inclined to remain in the new country. All sorts of new ties are developed that bind one to the new country, such as new country spouses, children, relatives, and so on. America gets further and further away emotionally and the migrants begin to view themselves as *vatikim* (veteran settlers) rather than as *olim hadashim* (new immigrants).

WORK AND HOUSING (QUADRANT B)

Yes, we didn't know enough about how "she'll be right" penetrates everything. "She'll be right" is focusing on the effect, but behind it is "don't do anything too well, because you'll show up your mates, you'll raise the quota too high, the overseer will beat us."

These are the words of Heather, a college graduate and employee of an Australian university, who is married with a preschool child. Such an observation is reinforced by a Sydney migration expert who discussed economic prospects for American emigrants in business with *Newsweek*.

Business is handled differently here. Australians don't like to be pushed into a deal. They place more importance on personal relationships. Americans are used to the hard sell and getting a deal done and closed. They find it strange that the Australian is not out there just to make a buck. (Meyer *et al.*, 1988, p. 52)

As *Newsweek*'s writers conclude, "Even in business—if you want to succeed, you have to relax and learn to say g'day" (Meyer *et al.*, 1988, p. 52).

Unlike the chapters on motivation where we began with quadrant A in which self-expressive concerns predominated, we begin here with quadrant B, self-instrumental issues, because they are most frequently mentioned by the emigrants.

Many Americans went to Australia expecting that the assumed common language and culture meant that what they would find would resemble American life. Perhaps the most frequently mentioned conflict of values centered on the American and Australian attitudes toward work. College-trained, professionally ambitious, socialized to be competitive, and imbued with the American work ethic, Americans frequently complained about the slower and, to them, mediocre standard of work in Australia. The Australian expression, "she'll be right," means one should not take things too seriously, for "it'll get done by and by." Thus, when one of the research team asked to get into the office to work on weekends (as had been the norm back in the States in graduate school), no one could understand why one would go to work on the weekend when it was not strictly required. Nobody else did, the Australians said; and migrants were not expected to either. (By the way, they gave us the key, but we never used it.)

Heather and John, for example, moved to Australia so that John could pursue his Ph.D. on a fellowship. Heather was already a university graduate, and while tending their preschool son managed to complete an advanced degree as well. They were both hardworking, professionally oriented academics, and had brought their American-ingrained ambition and standards of professionalism with them. Both were university-employed and had decided to defer returning to the States until the employment opportunities there improved. (They were well aware of the apparent glut of Ph.D.s on the marketplace that began to appear during the early 1970s.) Meanwhile, they intended to improve their professional qualifications so they could "market" themselves more advantageously when they returned. They had already been in Australia five years and could not guess when they might return to the States. Understandably, Heather rendered a somewhat intellectual summary of her adjustment difficulties. Particularly troublesome was her discovery that many Australians shared an anti-intellectual bias which, together with the unpressured Australian work ethic, made them feel isolated from the Australian mainstream. (Of course, they might have encountered this bias in Alabama, Alaska, or Arizona!) They had learned to cope by restricting their social and professional relationships to people who were as ambitious as they were, usually other expatriates. Their academic professions set them apart from most Australians, hindering their sense of assimilation. They had been socialized to a cosmopolitan life-style that they could not express in Australia.

We asked, "Did you think you knew enough to prepare you for coming here? Did you find any adjustments that you had to make, that you hadn't expected?" Heather replied:

> I don't know if I'm projecting this too much, but certainly there's a very strong feeling that you must not excel, and that goes into "she'll be right," and that means that my mail doesn't get delivered, and that my typing is done badly, and therefore I can't do my job. And being an American with a success orientation, I found that very hard. You have this conflict between doing your own job and liking your work. You're crazy if you like your work here. People think that I'm absolutely mad to do volunteer professional work. I get teased about being an American hustler. And all I can say is, "but all my friends do it at home."
>
> The anti-intellectuality in Australia is tied up with the convict past (Britain originally settled Australia as a prison colony), if you will, the looking down upon intellectual achievements as being a way to better things, and you've got to be careful not to better them because you might force them to do some work.
>
> I think it is a sociological truism that a feeling of belonging comes from conform-

ing with the norms of society in which you live, and that if you want to be what you were in the past, then you either have to keep to a very small subculture that has the norms that you believe in, that you've internalized, and this subculture is very small here. . . . Therefore, I probably feel lonelier here than in the same sort of city in the United States.

They also ask you where you are working, what do you do for your living and then it comes out that you've come out to work at the university. I'm also aware that when you say "university," that immediately sets you up in a class for an Australian. They'll type you so much faster. That's why I'm pleased with the American system where everybody has a college degree; and, therefore, everyone has a second chance. And when they say, "I've got a college degree," you don't immediately put them into an elite class and say, "Oh, I have to be careful now," or "Oh, he's one of my own." You have to find something else about the individual instead of being typecast as you are in Australia.

Even though not everyone in America has a college degree, Heather was expressing her feelings of isolation and being out of step with most Australians, even with Australian academic colleagues. Still longing to return to the States, Heather and John had not resolved the cultural dissimilarities. For Heather, this strain was sharper because she realized that she was violating dominant Australian gender role models. Even less than in the United States, Australians neither expect nor want women to assume managerial and leadership positions.

Adjusting to Australian working norms involved more than coping with "she'll be right." Americans found that seemingly similar Australian and American institutions did not, in fact, operate identically. American teachers, for instance, found that Australian schools were not entirely what they hoped or wanted them to be. By 1977 there were more than 1,200 of them in the state of Victoria (Bardo and Bardo, 1980a). As with Julie, Scott, and Pat, American migrant teachers were usually recent U.S. college graduates, facing a tight labor market (actually a glut of teachers), and yearning for independence. They were shocked that many Australian teenagers left school without graduating but with a "leavers" certificate, which was sufficient to qualify the 16-year-old for many semiskilled jobs without the stigma a "dropout" faces in the States. And they were often critical of the model of teaching they were required to follow, one that seemed authoritarian and aloof. Other researchers have found that

American and Australian teachers have different areas of concern . . . Australian teachers are expected to be more authoritarian, more conforming to systemic demands, less involved with interpersonal relations, more oriented to teacher-made rules, and much less permissive than their American counterparts. These differences in expectations were associated with a fair degree of dissatisfaction among American teachers in Victoria's schools, though there was a high degree of satisfaction with the teachers by administrators. (Bardo and Bardo, 1980a, p. 599)

Here, as with all other adjustments, what appeared to be a single adjustment was likely compounded by ongoing adjustments in other areas of daily living. Where everyday living was stress-free and "fluent," problems at work doubtless became less stressful. As Bardo and Bardo concluded, much of their apparent dissatisfaction grew out of their general problem of adjusting to a new way of life: "Much of the dissatisfaction noted in previous studies may be associated, at least in part, with general problems of adjustment and relocation" (1980a, p. 600).

Americans generally agreed that Australia's schools were excessively disciplinarian, rigid, and pedagogically backward. But eventually their expectations and standards changed, their children blended in, and the schools were no longer a problem. The teachers expected more autonomy in their classrooms and had been trained to try to personalize their instruction. Australian schools posed these and other more subtle differences. Still, they almost always learned to cope with the new way of doing things (and learned not to push too hard to change things to their liking!). We interviewed four teachers and did not find a common set of complaints about the system. Two found Australian schools professionally dissatisfying places to work. But they all deeply appreciated having a job, given the restricted opportunities for teaching in the States at the time. And given that it provided the opportunity to travel around the world, they thought they had a good job. Some discovered that teaching in Australia did have intrinsic satisfaction. Julie thought she could make a difference. And finally, they all found themselves fitting in comfortably with Australian life and discovering life-styles that they were learning to like.

Americans complained about other work-related difficulties. Skilled workers did not always find their qualifications and credentials honored (although American college and post-college degrees found ready acceptance). This meant "starting over" (apprenticeship, journeyman, union card). Certainly the low pay for the same work they had been doing in the States was a status-threatening experience for many. Americans in supervisory positions over Australians required a kind of tact that was unnecessary in the States. Australians did not appreciate American go-getters and resisted American supervision.

Most of the Americans we interviewed had stayed long enough to have gone beyond frustration and had grown to appreciate the Australian approach to work. They liked the fact that there was much less competition in the Australian economy. Finding and keeping a job was less of a pressure than in the States. Trained to American competitive standards and norms, Americans learned that the relaxed Australian attitude about work relieved an enormous source of pressure. The informality of dress and interaction, the opportunities for anyone with some degree of ambition, perhaps the chance to be "a one-eyed king in the land of the blind," as Steve put it, all were important satisfactions that helped neutralize the less attractive side of working in Australia.

Many Americans internalized the relaxed Australian work ethic and came to regard it as a valued feature of Australia's quality of life. Work was a particularly important concern to men, whose social roles were heavily intertwined with occupational roles. When work was satisfactory, Americans could find Australia a comfortable place to live.

> By far the most often mentioned disliked aspects of Australian life were the wage structure and the cost of living. In general, interviewees felt that there existed considerable disparity between salaries and the cost of living and, although many had been prepared for a reduction in money income, they had not expected a cost of living which they felt was very much comparable to that in the United States.
>
> In summary, the majority (4 out of 5) felt that their expectations about Australia had been met and in some cases exceeded. Where disappointments were expressed, they generally involved the disparity between the wages and the cost of living to which a number had found it hard to adjust. (Australian Department of Labour and Immigration, 1971, pp. 46, 48)

One reason many Americans moved to Australia was because they perceived that the Australian standard of living seemed particularly compatible with what they enjoyed at home: electricity, highways, automobiles, modern appliances, modern department stores, and American products and companies everywhere they looked. Our survey showed that one in four respondents (24%) felt their standard of living was worse or much worse in Australia than in the States, while another quarter (28%) considered it better or much better. Nearly half (46%) said it was pretty much the same.

Really significant adjustments, however, were more cultural than material. Core values and normative expectations of Americans and Australians often contradicted each other. The 1971 Australian government study offered the following conclusion about the Americans who had been reinterviewed:

> Although the group of Americans interviewed could be said to be relatively free of the basic settlement problems outlined above (" . . . in the areas of accommodation, employment, and social/communication . . . few demands were made upon official and other sources of assistance"), they did appear to face some problems nevertheless. These problems were concerned with the basic differences between American and Australian society—economically, socially, culturally, and in other ways. Fundamentally, interviewees were faced with a need to adjust to a generally less highly developed society operating at different levels of economic and social activity. For some, the change appeared to be a welcome one; but for others the adjustments required were too great . . . for some interviewees the generally slower and more relaxed pace of life in Australia and other "credits" appeared to offset or at least balance the economic and other "debits," but for others, including those for whom the economic drive was still prominent, this did not appear to be the case. (Australian Department of Labour and Immigration, 1971, p. 10)

The complaints encountered in Israel were not all that different from Australia. Not all emigrants were prepared for what they encountered. For example, Yussi, a particularly frustrated migrant, complained that what he actually found when he settled in Israel was very much different from what he had come to expect from all his visits as a tourist. To try and express his feeling he told a clerk in the Ministry of Absorption the following joke:

> To help him decide whether to live a life of sin or a life of virtue, Sam decided to make a tour of Heaven and Hell to see what would await him. Everyone in Heaven was sitting around rickety tables and reading religious books. It looked very boring. The picture in Hell was entirely different—wild parties and drinking. Everyone was having a grand time. The choice was clear. But lo and behold, upon his death, after living a life of sin what did he actually encounter in Hell? Fire and Brimstone! When he complained to Hell's Minister of Absorption and asked why it was so different from what he saw when he had come to visit, the answer was, "Last time you were a tourist."

Yussi said what was amazing to him was that the clerk could not understand the moral of the story. He told him, "if you think it's better there, then go to Hell!"

The first major problem that Americans moving to a new country would seem to have is just deciding where to live. This is less of a problem for many Americans in Israel because preparations for the move are facilitated by immigration offices in the United States. For example, many Americans have taken up initial residence in an absorption center that may also double as a Hebrew language training center. The advantage of this arrangement is that immigrants can learn Hebrew, look for a job, and decide where to live once they have found a place of employment. Other Americans do move, initially into rented apartments.

Purchasing an apartment is probably the single greatest expenditure that Americans in Israel have to face. Almost all residences are in condominium buildings. The decision of where to live is affected by instrumental as well as expressive considerations. Instrumentally, there is the question of balancing one's desire to live in proximity to one's work with the fact that desirable apartments closer to the center of a major city are also the more expensive ones. Expressive considerations relate to finding a community and neighborhood that is socially suitable.

The high cost of an apartment is more of a burden on young, single persons who come as temporary residents and decide to stay than it is on older persons who more often initially immigrated on a permanent basis. This is due to a self-selection process. Older migrants move with a greater understanding of the costs involved. Therefore, if they cannot afford the costs, they do not move. The younger migrants more often move despite the costs, trusting that their parents and family members will assist them later on. For example, Nadja, a Zionist from early on, says that she did not really know how she could afford to live in Israel, but assumed that she would manage like native Israelis do—by having one's parents help her. She came as a single woman, eventually married, and sure enough, got her parents to buy her a nice apartment in Jerusalem.

For some Americans, finding work is quite problematic. Many Americans in Israel seek employment in the professions. There are many American doctors, lawyers, accountants, and university professors throughout the country. However, there are also a substantial number of entrepreneurs. Some open ice-cream stores, fast-food establishments, and even repair shops. The Association of American and Canadians in Israel regularly publishes a bulletin in which some of these persons advertise, emphasizing that they speak English and that they provide service "like it should be" (and as it was back in the States). The U.S.-based Association of Parents of North Americans in Israel also publishes a newsletter encouraging Americans in Israel to utilize the services of their children in Israel.

One of the problems that Americans in Israel encounter is the constant inefficiency. Consider the mail service. At the time of this study it regularly took a week for a letter to be delivered between its two largest cities, Tel Aviv and Jerusalem—which are just 45 miles apart. Airmail letters regularly take ten days to travel between Israel and the United States. This is hardly understandable, given the fact that there are generally two direct flights a day between Tel Aviv and New York. To overcome this problem, tourists and visitors are regularly asked to mail letters in the other country when traveling abroad. When large numbers of American migrants are concentrated in one particular area in Israel, an organized system occasionally develops to identify couriers who are willing to take part in what amounts to a self-help program. For example, Americans in one religious residential project who intend to travel to the United States announce their departure date on a sign-up sheet posted in the local synagogue. One of the conditions of these self-help systems is that the American postage be affixed by the sender in Israel, and postage stamps are one of the many staples that Americans in Israel stock up on when visiting the United States.

There is inefficiency to be found in all walks of life. Construction work appears to be sloppy and to necessitate constant supervision by a residential buyer. Ruthie, who built a very expensive private villa in the heart of Tel Aviv, tells of how she imported an exquisitely carved wood door for her house only to come home one day and find it slopped over with white paint. A painter working on the house forgot what he was supposed to paint and he figured it was better to paint too much than too little. She figured she would soak away her anger in a hot bath, only to find that the plumber had installed the bathtub the wrong way in her absence.

The problem of inefficiency, bureaucracy, and a general lackadaisical attitude toward work standards is particularly hard on the immigrants who are trying to build up a small enterprise and make a contribution to Israel at the same time. Yussi, our settler with a sense of humor, complained that as a result of the inefficiency, bureaucracy, and unpredictable strikes, he could never be sure that the supplies that he needed for his small factory, which produced raincoats, would be delivered on time or would be of sufficient quality to meet his needs.

The interview with Yussi was conducted on a weekday morning because he was out of work. He had closed down his factory and was in the process of deciding whether to remain in Israel.

COMMUNITY AND BELONGING (QUADRANT A)

"Everytime somebody blinks their eye, there's a holiday in Australia," perhaps best summarizes the views of Ed, who was retired from a lifetime in show business, on his adjustment to Australia. Starting as a radio announcer in New York before World War II, he moved to Hollywood, where the pressures associated with his work led to his alcoholism. This eventually helped to convince him to move to Sydney with his Australian-born wife, Cass. Adjustment was not as easy as his father-in-law had led him to expect, but he managed to slow down to the Australian pace of life. They lived in a modest ranch-style house in an outer suburb of Melbourne. Cass joined us for the interview, but Ed did all the talking. He liked to talk, and his memory spilled over with an astonishing series of dates, people, and anecdotes (e.g., "I got Chet Huntley into news announcing"), but he concluded:

> I worried when I first came out here whether I could adjust to the slower pace. And the first 6 months, I will admit, were a bit trying on me. I was impatient to get things done. It would take 10 days here where it would take 15 minutes for a decision in the States. But after I'd been here, the slower pace, the easier way of life, and friendliness of the people . . . I was lucky I was accepted very quickly.

How did you adapt?

> I slowed down, without realizing it, which I think has saved my life. Took me nine months. I had slowed down to the tempo of Australian life, that's what it amounted to. I said, "Well, this is for me." To this day I can't get used to the holidays they have in Australia. Everytime somebody blinks their eye, there's a holiday in Australia.
>
> The hardest thing of all, in an 8 hour day, the average Australian would not work more than 6 hours . . . smoke breaks, tea breaks, or coffee breaks, they would not work more than 6 hours a day. It seemed like I would be right in the middle of something and they'd say, "it's time for tea." Used to drive me crazy, twice a day they had tea or coffee break. Your tea break would be at least 30 minutes, 45 minutes, having a little chat about everything in general, some of it was good for business, most wasn't. That annoyed me.

Most Americans we talked with would instantly recognize Ed's frustrations with the easygoing Australian lifestyle. As accepting of Australia as he was, Ed could still find much to criticize; after 25 years, he still found himself adjusting to cultural differences. But as he frequently asserted, the adjustments were manageable and the rewards of living there were more than enough to compensate for the inconveniences.

American migrants do not form an "ethnic community" in Australia. In fact, typically they do not socialize with fellow Americans at all. A few reported that at first they sought out Americans for friendships, largely because of loneliness. Teachers especially reported that they formed early friendships with other American teachers whom they had met on the trip to Australia. A few of the interviewed migrants sought American companionship through such social organizations as the Australian-American Association. But the search for other Americans became less and less important as Yanks became increasingly involved in the diverse activities of daily living and especially as friendships with Australians emerged through typical channels—parties, work, other friends. Overall, 47% of the Yanks in our survey claimed they had no American friends in Australia, 30% said they had only 1 or 2, and only 6% claimed 11 or more. Most found that making friends with Australians was fairly easy, as 42% of the Yanks claimed 11 or more Australian friends. Increasingly, the importance of friendships became based on fundamental personality similarities, rather than shared identities as Americans.

Those most strongly oriented to return to America were more likely to have numerous American friends than those who did not pay the matter much concern. Nearly half (48%) of the settlers (those who said they would stay six years or longer) claimed no American friends and 21% said they had three or more American friends. Of the returnees (those intending to return in five years or less), 38% claimed three or more American friends.

For Jewish Americans who decided to "come home" to Israel, the need for expressive adjustment may come as a surprise. The fact that they are not immediately accepted as "native Israelis" makes them realize that while they came as Jews, they are in effect Americans. Their way of life is different, as are their cultural norms. The problems of inefficiency and bureaucracy impede more than instrumental adjustment. They indicate a different orientation to a whole lifestyle. The reaction to an attempt to implement a more efficient mail procedure can easily be viewed as "you're still an American." Indeed, this is one reason why seminars on culture shock have been organized for new immigrants. Once they get over the euphoria of their initial move and begin to settle down, they realize that not everything is as rosy as they first thought.

A particularly interesting group has been formed by local chapters of the Association of Americans and Canadians in Israel for Americans married to Israelis. These groups are by and large composed of American women married to Israeli men who must struggle with the difficulty of adjusting to Israeli norms and expectations not only in more formal settings outside the home, but in the home as well. Many of the persons who join these groups have little family of their own in Israel, and thus they are not only marrying an Israeli male, but are also entering a total family situation that is thoroughly Israeli. The cultural adaptation required is quite pronounced.

With extraordinary candor, Rivkah, who married an Israeli man, told us about her dissatisfaction with her husband's Israeli standards of cleanliness, his patronizing attitude toward women, and his demand to have food prepared and served "like we Israelis do it, not like you Americans." She said that if she could just go down the block to her mother and sisters once in a while, she would be able to take the situation much better. But her family lives 8,000 miles away.

There is one requirement in Israel that leads to a sense of belonging and that is military service. Most older male immigrants are recruited for only an abbreviated term in consideration of their age. Younger immigrants, who probably are more eager to feel Israeli than older persons, can serve a regular three-year stint. Married women do not serve, and thus young couples who migrate can theoretically expect to have the man spend some time in military service while his wife remains home waiting for his visits. While this is a positive feature for the husband, it can be a negative one for his wife who may not have many friends to keep her company and with whom she can visit while she is by herself.

One pattern of social adjustment for many Americans is to consciously seek out other American friends, often by moving to areas known to have a high concentration of Americans. Jerusalem, for example, attracts many religious immigrants, and many of them are Americans. There are some communities that have such a high number of English-speaking residents that one can argue, sociologically, that the residents are living in a transposed American community. Such areas exist in a number of suburban cities surrounding Tel Aviv. It is not necessary for a particular community to be composed of only Americans. On the contrary, having Israeli neighbors enables the immigrant to feel that he or she is becoming integrated in Israeli society. However, a critical mass of Americans in the neighborhood enables many migrants to develop a social network composed of other Americans.

One might think that these Americans socializing with other Americans would feel that they are outsiders in Israeli society. The contrary is the case. Those Americans who live in residential areas that are primarily composed of native Israelis can see themselves as outsiders to a still greater degree. For example, David, an outgoing American, married an Israeli woman and lives in an all-Israeli neighborhood. He complains that he just does not belong. He is just not part of the clique of Israelis in the neighborhood as much as he tries. "We just don't have a common language." Such persons come to feel like outsiders in Israel.

On the other hand, those Americans who socialize with other "Americans" are affiliating with other Olim. For their purpose, they are affiliating with other "new Israelis" like themselves. In such circumstances they become the insiders. Indeed, in their talks and discussions they talk about "them" and "us" meaning "Americans in the United States" and "we Israelis." And when entertaining American tourists they will talk about "you" and "us."

Yet, many of these Americans are cut off from mainstream Israeli culture. Language is a primary barrier. For example, while many Americans learn Hebrew well, few are comfortable enough in it to read Hebrew novels or the Hebrew press. Many read the English-language *Jerusalem Post*, which, unlike the Hebrew-language papers, provides expansive coverage of American sports events; many listen to English-language news on the radio, broadcast three times a day, rather than to the hourly Hebrew news broadcasts.

One setting in which Americans affiliate with other Americans, and more broadly with other Anglo-Saxons, is in the synagogue. Some Orthodox synagogues tend to attract many Anglo-Saxons, especially the "Young Israel" movement synagogues which originated in the United States. Additionally, many Reform and Conservative synagogues have a high proportion of Americans as members, including some who did not attend services on a regular basis prior to moving to Israel. To some extent, these synagogues serve an ethnic function in addition to the religious function that they provide their members (Tabory and Lazerwitz, 1983).

Some degree of social segregation, then, enables the American immigrants to feel that they have achieved what they wanted—to identify as Israelis in their adopted land. To some extent, their affiliation with other Americans enables them to gloss over their dissimilarity with "native Israelis." They take as a reference group Americans who did not move to Israel so that by contrast they can characterize themselves as Israelis.

The upshot of this discussion is that a sense of community and belonging is very important to these immigrants precisely because it is for this reason that they came to Israel. Satisfaction of instrumental needs is a necessary condition for "making it" in Israel, but less than total instrumental adaptation is also tolerable, if the expressive satisfaction for the self meets or exceeds the levels of such expectations that one had prior to migration.

FAMILY UNITY AND SOLIDARITY (QUADRANT C)

In this quadrant the adjustment challenges are focused on relationships with others, such as family and friends. Australia was a long way from home (about 11,000 miles from New York and 24 hours flying time). We felt sure when we began the study that we would find this distance to be daunting and troublesome to American migrants. Bardo and Bardo (1980a) have noted that the feeling of being cut off from home was a relatively serious adjustment problem facing Americans, especially for women.

The people we interviewed, however, rarely felt this way. There were those who recalled feeling lonely and far away from home. But they soon found ways to cope with these feelings. One way of adjusting was to become convinced that home was just a 24-hour flight away. Males and females alike seemed to take the distance in stride. Where they differed was in their yearning for distant family and friends.

The real significance of distance, of course, is the physical separation from loved ones. Does the separation cause problems of adjustment, loneliness, homesickness, or feelings of being cut off? However it is called, missing social intimates can make life abroad unhappy. It seems that female migrants felt the absence of friends and family more sharply than did males. Or, perhaps they were just more willing to reveal such feelings. Women were more likely than men to recall adjustments to social absence, as Bardo and Bardo have also noted. This, no doubt, reflected the differences in value men and women placed on such ties. Women considered them more important, depended on them as a regular part of daily life, and were, therefore, more likely to miss their loss. Men were more generally socialized to self-reliance and independence, expected to leave home and travel widely, and leave friends and family behind.

> Thus, it appears that women's attitudes toward the educational system (that is, the major work place) and their feelings of belonging are affected by how well their husbands adjust to life in Australia. . . . Further, in the previous research on American teachers, it was noted that males and females differed significantly in the degree to which they missed their old relationships in the U.S.A. No such differences were found among married teachers. This result suggests that it is among single people that there are the greatest sex-role-related differences. It is logical that the marital relationship provides outlets for at least some of these familistic feelings and, thereby, may aid over-all adjustment. (Bardo and Bardo, 1981, p. 627)[1]

Some female Yanks explained how they felt about being so far from friends and family. Julie was asked how she felt about Australia being the other end of the world: "At that particular time in my life it looked damned good. Thousands of miles away from him (her ex-husband) was good. That sounds terrible but that is the way I felt." "How about friendships?" the interviewer asked. "Oh, that's the hard part. My very best friend still lives there. I still feel very badly."

Chris spoke on the same subject:

> I had . . . leaving my family and all those sort of feelings, but nothing strong enough to have swayed the decision. I knew that I had to come. . . . My father was very ill at the time, he had cancer and he was in remission and they didn't know whether he would live or not. But I reasoned that he wouldn't want me to wait around for him to die before I started to go out and live my life, and that I could fly back if I needed to be there.

Maizie was asked whether moving was a big step for her: "It wasn't. But I think it was a bigger step probably . . . I realized it was a bigger step once I arrived, when the boat set out and I was far away." Interviewer: "Did the distance from here to Chicago influence you at all? Did you ever think about how far away it was?"

> Yah, I did, I think I finally realized how far away it was by the fact that it took me a month to get here. No, no, it's only a matter of money, isn't it? It doesn't make any difference if it's here to Sydney or here to Chicago, really. If you've got that much money, then you can go.

---

[1]Based on a very small sample, the Australian Department of Labour and Immigration's Survey of U.S. Immigrants, Phase II, noted that " . . . young single females had a much higher departure rate than had young single males" (1971, p. 3). This is the opposite of what occurs in Israel.

Women were aware of these social ties and regretted their weakening or loss. But with only one exception, nobody said they wanted to return in order to be with friends and family. Being without friends and family was significant mostly for those who found it difficult to integrate into Australian daily life, people without satisfying employment or family bonds within Australia. Many women seemed more anxious about their families' feelings than their own. They often realized that their Stateside relationships were no longer as significant as their new ties in Australia.

Karen reported on her ties to family and friends: "I had convinced myself that I wasn't coming out permanently, at least I didn't consider it a permanent stay until after I got here. In fact I think I set an arbitrary period of one year in my mind." The interviewer continued: "When you got here, did you write to many people, correspond with friends?"

> Oh, this getting . . . this is striking home. I just know what you are getting at and it's not why it suddenly rings a bell with me . . . but I just sent a Christmas letter home this year and I found it very difficult, wrenching, because I realized how few people there are left.

Females, it appears, did miss their families and friends more than males did.[2] They talked about homesickness, especially during the early stage after their arrival in Australia. Men also had to cope with distance from significant social ties to friends and family, too, of course; and many of them discussed the pains of separation from a special friend or a desire to be closer to family (almost always meaning parents). The cure for loneliness was involvement in work, in making friends with Australians (rarely with other Americans), participating in the new life-style, and exploring the new country. The search for adventure that had brought most of them to Australia necessarily required that social ties to home be suspended. Knowing this and expecting it to be only temporary, most found the loss of intimate contacts manageable, if not always pleasant. But regardless of their reasons for going to Australia, no migrants indicated that they wanted to return because they could not adjust to the loss of friends and family. And the reason for this is related to the initial migrant intentions.

Family unity is a problematic issue for some of the migrants to Israel. In some cases of international migration, the migrant emigrates in order to get away from family and friends. The severance of family ties allows the migrant the freedom to do what he or she would like to do—to start anew elsewhere unfettered by past ties. There are some cases like that in migration to Israel, but they are not the norm. By and large the American migrants come despite the strong ties that they had with their American families and friends. The degree to which these persons are missed can become apparent only after awhile.

---

[2]One study that has explored in depth the adjustment experiences of immigrant women did not treat the issue of the loss of family and friendship ties (Evans, 1984).

In an interview about this topic, Gloria, a woman in her late 30s with several Israeli-born children, emphasized the difficulty of being away from her sisters and her parents:

> I love my husband and my children, and it is because of that that I want us to have a real family life. That includes my family back home. If it is difficult for me, it is even more difficult for them. The most we can do is write often, but it is not enough. I can't afford to call them often, let alone travel to visit them.

Gloria is lucky because her husband is also an American, and they speak English at home. The result is that their children can speak English as well as Hebrew. Sam's children, however, speak only Hebrew, and that makes it very difficult for the American grandparents.

> They come here to visit once a year, and it is a real problem. They weren't happy about my moving here to begin with, and now they can't really get all the enjoyment from their grandchildren like they deserve. I mean they can't really communicate with them, since my kids don't know English and they don't know Hebrew. My folks don't understand how I could do this to them.

As in Australia, being away from family seems to have a greater impact on women than men. There is some question whether this problem of adjustment is best considered as "self-expressive" or "others-expressive," but in order to compensate for the lack of close family ties in Israel, the immigrants seem to forge their own "make-believe" family—with other immigrants. One of the authors and his spouse were once introduced to a friend's parents in the following manner: "I've written you about them, mom, that they're like family to us here; so I wanted you to meet your other son and daughter."

One manner in which immigrants overcome the distance from their American families is quite simply by traveling back and forth between the two countries. Those who can afford the time and cost do so. It is quite common on New York-bound planes to see several mothers traveling with several small children on their way to the United States to show them off to grandparents, aunts, uncles, and cousins.

A more common pattern is for grandparents to travel to Israel to visit their Israeli families. There are also a substantial number of elderly couples in Israel who have moved there in order to be with some of their children. Others have moved there to retire, and spend several months of the year in the other country (Israel or the United States). For some, this is the best of two worlds—being able to spend time with each of their children or family members. For others, no matter where they are, it means that they are not somewhere else at that time.

Rarely did we encounter persons who spoke of their children's expressive needs in their own adjustment to Israel. The children generally managed to manage—it was the parents who did not. However, there were a few cases in which persons who came with older children expressed their doubt about their move because their children were not entirely happy. In one case a daughter, who moved to Israel for her sophomore year in high school, did not manage to integrate with an Israeli life-style, even though she served in the military upon her graduation. The parents wanted to stay in Israel for their own expressive reasons and decided to send their daughter to an American university, despite the high tuition and fees and the fact that she would be so far away from them.

SERVICE TO OTHERS (QUADRANT D)

Relocating to Australia to serve the instrumental goals of another person or organization was the least significant motive of all, and there are too few cases to permit confident generalizations. Therefore, the findings we present need to be cautiously interpreted. The experiences of Lisa and Tom reveal one mode of adjustment, perhaps the most benign as well. They were transferred by Tom's employer, Goodyear, after a three-year stint in Germany. They expected and relished a life-style of travel, and knew they would spend no more than two or three years at any assignment. Thus, they had already internalized an ethic of adjustment to whatever country they encountered by the time they arrived in Melbourne. After a somewhat difficult acculturation experience in Germany (neither spoke German fluently), they were very happy to find themselves in an English-speaking country with relatively familiar culture and institutions. Australia was gratifyingly easy to get used to, as Lisa explained:

> We'd already gone through a much more significant adjustment in moving to Germany. That took a long time to get used to. There is just a bigger cultural difference between the USA and Germany than the USA and here. One of the things that surprised me the most is how much Australia seems to be like the States. To be an American here is a little bit of a status symbol here, which it never was in Europe. There are just the adjustments of moving, the adjustments of new products, new brand names, the problems of running a household, different names for things. There's a slight language difference here. You tend to think of it when little phrases or words slip by, and you notice that you might not know what that means.

Their easy adjustment was due in large part to Tom's high salary and Goodyear's other generous financial benefits, such as cost of living salary enhancements. They lived in a spacious house outside of Melbourne and enjoyed a comfortable life-style. But more important was their determination to adjust gracefully to wherever they were transferred, knowing they would not have long before another relocation. While Tom and Lisa were technically emigrants according to the standard definition, they never had to deal with the possibility of whether to remain or return and all that implied for adjustment.

Instrumental adjustment plays an interesting role in the absorption process in Israel for some families. Essentially, heads of households exert their judgment regarding the absorption process for other members of their families. For example, as advanced as medical service is in Israel, it does not quite rate with the treatment available in top American medical establishments, and we encountered two cases of persons who returned to the United States because they felt members of their family needed long-term American medical care.

An additional consideration for family members is military service. It is one thing for a parent to join the military (and expressively benefit from such service, as far as his Israeli identity goes). It is another to require one's children to undertake a three-year stint in an army that can appear to be constantly under attack. We encountered several cases in which this factor was given as part of the reason for deciding to leave, but generally it was combined with more self-instrumental reasons, like the lack of suitable employment.

In only a few cases did we find evidence of individuals having difficulty in adjustment because of the instrumental needs of others. Such concerns focused on corporate transfers, military service, or medical care.

SUMMARY

As one well-known emigrant in the entertainment world, Stanley Kubrick, recently observed, rapid means of communication have reduced the physical and emotional distance, which in turn decreases the difficulty in adjusting to emigration. This chapter introduced the reader to an understanding of the nature of these adaptations.

Americans emigrated to Australia with the expectations that there would be few major adjustments. Many had visited before and observed the many surface similarities. They explained that first appearances could be deceiving, and by their second year they discovered the "real Australia." The Americans found little disruption to their employment in contrast to emigrants from Southern and Eastern Europe, who also faced much hostility from the natives. Indeed, Americans were highly regarded as a group.

Most Yanks (80%) reported there was at least one area of their life requiring a significant adjustment. The standard of living was lower, and strikes were more common. The work ethic was more lackadaisical, and the culture was macho-oriented. While some adjustments were difficult for some individuals, in general the similarities made it fairly easy for Yanks to adapt to Australia.

Expectations for Australia to be a quaint Americanized Anglo society were paralleled by Americans in Israel expecting to find an indigenous, authentic Jewish culture. As such, Olim, who worked outside the home, were nearly twice as satisfied with their work situation than other migrants, but were only one half as likely to state they were certain to stay in Israel. This is so despite the fact that Americans were highly regarded by Israeli society (as was true in Australia), had an enjoyable social life, developed contacts with native-born Israelis, and were acquiring a command of Hebrew.

The factors in adjustment to migration are not the same as those explaining motivation. Whereas, expressive concerns (quadrants A and C) dominated in propelling migration, instrumental issues (quadrant B) were preeminent in adapting to their new country. Concerns over housing, work, and the bureaucracy had to be resolved initially. Once these immediate issues are resolved, one can turn to finding friends, education, and a sense of satisfaction. These instrumental and expressive adjustments are based on a network of new social relationships and interpersonal contacts that link the emigrants to their new society. The easier the adjustments, the stronger the social ties and emotional identification with the host society.

Americans moving abroad, whether to Australia or Israel, need to adjust to a lower standard of living. This adjustment together with the perception of a more lackadaisical work ethic pose serious challenges for Americans to stay abroad. Despite these difficulties, a considerable proportion endure, remain, and prosper.

The emigrants came largely for expressive reasons, but subsequent to migration, individuals have to deal with the instrumental concerns and the issues of quadrant B (work and housing) and to a much lesser extent quadrant D (service to others). Subsequent to dealing with these instrumental issues, they encounter the expressive challenges posed in quadrants A and C (community and belonging and family unity and solidarity).

As the emigrants go through the different aspects of the migration process, they face different decisions. The first is whether to migrate and the second is whether to remain or return. The challenges to adjustment presented in this chapter represent the waves between these twin shores of decision making. In this process the individuals need to become different social persons in order to overcome successfully each decision hurdle. The struggles posed in this process lead ultimately to the question faced by the emigrants—whether to remain in their new country or return home—which is examined in the next chapters.

6

Toward a Model of the Migration Cycle

> We used to call it, our Monday-Wednesday-Friday; we would think of going back to
> the States; and on Tuesday-Thursday-Saturday, we would think about staying. . . . On
> Sunday we wouldn't care.

Perhaps this reflection by one of our Australian respondents best characterizes the experience of the emigrants once they have arrived in their adopted country. They must confront the issue of whether to remain or return. For some it is a constant preoccupation and for others there is a perennial ambivalence. On what bases does the act of staying as opposed to leaving rest?

The statistically richer data on the migrants to Israel permit us to begin to answer this question. Secondary analysis of a panel study differentiates between those who stayed in Israel for at least three years and those who left. While the data on migrants to Australia do not enable us to differentiate completely between stayers and leavers, they do provide an initial indication of who will and who will not remain.

The Australian data permitted separating these migrants into sojourners and settlers. As the prior discussion of these two social categories showed, sojourners appear to be much more likely to leave than settlers. Hence, looking at the differences between them will give us a good sense of why many of these migrants returned to the United States. When this is done, it will be possible to contrast Australian with Israeli differences. By so doing, it will be feasible to generalize across both groups of American migrants.

Table 6.1 enables us to draw these conclusions about those who stay with regard to those who leave:

1. Arriving married, getting married, and getting married to a citizen of the new country clearly promotes staying there.

101

Table 6.1. Comparisons of American Migrants to Australia and Israel

		Migrants to	
	Factors	Australia	Israel
1.	Sex ratio	Settlers are about 60% men; sojourners split 50–50.	Stayers are about 60% women; leavers split 50–50.
2.	Marital status	About 34% of the settlers were never married; 45% of the sojourners were never married.	23% of the stayers were never married; 41% of the leavers were never married.
3.	Current marital status	Just 14% of settlers were single while 38% of the sojourners were single.	After 3 years, 14% of the stayers were single while 34% of the leavers were single.
4.	Standard of living: U.S. vs. new country (for Israel, satisfaction with current economic situation)	Just 22% of settlers claim Australian standard worse than U.S. while 38% of sojourners say it is worse.	78% of stayers were satisfied with current economic situation and 77% of leavers were satisfied.
5.	Sense of adventure behind migration	Just 50% of the settlers say that a sense of adventure was important for their migration while 70% of the sojourners say it was important.	This type of question was not asked.
6.	Importance of work options	37% of settlers said that Australian work options were important for their migration in contrast to 51% of the sojourners.	Question not asked.
7.	Presence of family ties	39% of the settlers said that Australian family ties were important in their migration while 19% of the sojourners said this.	Question not asked.
8.	Self-perception as more at home in new country than in U.S.	28% of settlers felt they were more Australian than American while just 4% of the sojourners felt this way.	33% of the stayers felt that they were more Israeli than American while only 20% of the leavers felt this way.

2. While comparable Israeli data are absent, it is quite likely for both groups of migrants that having family ties in the new country (apart from marriage) promotes staying over leaving.
3. Those who stay are more satisfied with their job and standard of living than are those who leave.
4. Those who migrate out of a sense of adventure are also the ones most likely to leave, and those who move with certain religioethnic convictions and experiences are more likely to stay.
5. Those who do stay perceive themselves as more at home in their new country than in the United States.
6. Sex ratios are not the same for both groups. Americans going to Australia include more men than women while the opposite applies to Americans going to Israel. Again, men and women are about equally divided among the transients and among those who leave Israel.

These conclusions about staying versus leaving are rather simple ones. Later in this chapter, we shall see that more advanced statistical analysis of the American migrants to Israel indicates that the staying-leaving set of factors are more complex than expected and that questions like those discussed here are limited in explaining a great deal about who stays or who leaves. The set of factors that causes one to migrate from the United States is not the same set of factors that determines social experiences after arrival in the new country and that affects the decision to stay or leave.

Most American migrants to Australia were in fact sojourners, going for an extended time, a matter of years perhaps. Eventually most have returned to America. For some, as they became more involved in daily living, it became easier and easier to put their Stateside relationships behind them, until they discovered, as Karen in Australia did, that they were writing only once a year, or every other year—and not even realizing that it had come to that. Ties to friends and family in America could pose problems of loneliness and homesickness, but migrants, including female migrants, generally managed to cope with their "temporary" loss.

Settlers faced a somewhat different problem since they thought they were leaving their Stateside relationships for good. Most felt they would visit home sometime, or perhaps a friend or parent might visit them in Australia. But most visits would be short. Normal life would never include their friends and families back home. This was sometimes a wrenching realization, and we may never know how many would-be settlers changed their minds and returned to the United States because of their reluctance to lose these relationships. But those who pursued their goal of migration and settlement already had learned to cope with these losses. Many, for instance, had resolved to return for a parent's convalescence from an illness or to attend a parent's funeral. It was not "forever gone" in their minds. Others noted that even a relocation within the States would have involved similar pangs of separation, with only occasional visits, and weakened ties of friendships. We do not think any migrant, settler or sojourner, considered such losses as irrevocable. America was only a plane ride home. For many, the rewards of the new life—as entrepreneur or as spouse—were more than enough to balance these losses.

Americans usually found that accepting Australian life was easy, even fun to do. They had anticipated that the two cultures would be compatible, although they knew they would have to put up with some discomfort. After all, that was part of the adventure of living abroad, posing more of a challenge than a threat. Material differences, such as a lower standard of living and new foods, were probably easier to deal with than were more subtle cultural differences, because they were more visible and could be neutralized. High earnings (compared with the general Australian wage scale) insulated many Yanks from material hardships. But differences in values often posed deeper problems in the long run, largely because it took awhile even to realize these differences existed. So much of Australian life seemed familiar that many Yanks fooled themselves into thinking there were no differences at all. It took time for them to realize how the Australian work ethic clashed with their own American "Puritan Ethic," and to realize how deeply embedded their values of competition and toil were rooted. It took time to realize how thoroughly the Australian male working-class culture was embedded in Australian society. Few Americans could entirely forget that in the eyes of Australians, they would always be Yanks, no matter how long they lived there as it is very difficult for emigrants who are teens or older to drop their accents. Becoming Australian would take a lifetime.

Settlers and sojourners alike found it easy to fit in, to find acceptance by Australian friends and employers, and to function smoothly within Australian institutions. They could suspend their ties to family and friends in America without actually destroying them. After all, most felt that they would return to the States (indeed they did), and accepted "temporary" weakened ties as a normal part of life anyway. But as life in Australia became easier, even normal for some, their thoughts of returning grew dimmer and less frequent. Their already weak integration into Stateside community, family, and work had permitted them to move abroad in the first place. Now that they were in Australia, new commitments grew stronger and stronger, filling the void of weaker and weaker links to American society. Most settlers resolved to stay, and some sojourners were turning into settlers.

As in the case of the Yanks, an understanding of the issue of staying or leaving among the Olim requires separating them into different categories. The Immigrant Absorption panel survey indicates that of the original 560 respondents 63% (called "stayers") remained and 37% (called "leavers") left by the end of the three-year panel period.[1] Of these, 21% left during the first panel year; another 9% left during the second panel year; and 7% left during the third year.

The staying percentage for Yanks drops from the first census period onward throughout the approximately 20 years under review. Note, however, that the decrease is a substantial 18% for Yanks from 1961 to 1975 but appears to slow down for the 1976 to 1981 period. (The staying rates for both settlers and sojourners are quite similar.) Over a period of 20 years, 25% of American migrants to Australia appear to be staying there.

For American Olim going to Israel, an opposite pattern appears. The initial ten-year staying rate was 42%. However, during the second part of the 20-year period it has improved to an overall rate for the two decades of 48%. Finally, the three-year staying rate was 63% for the migrants of the panel study years of 1969 to 1971. Of course, this figure is higher because it covers a much shorter period of time.

THE MODEL OF THE MIGRATION CYCLE

Table 6.2 presents some major behavioral and attitudinal characteristics of the adjustment-absorption process of the stayers and leavers at various stages based on the data from the Israeli sample. These characteristics can be sorted into three types: satisfactions, contacts, and perceptions.

After two months, stayers were more likely than leavers to be quite satisfied economically and to be slightly more likely to be "well" or "quite" satisfied with their social life, their housing, and their Hebrew. Throughout the three-year panel period the stayers displayed stability in their social and housing satisfactions. By the end of their first year in Israel, stayers increased their satisfaction with Hebrew progress and remained fairly stable afterward. Their economic satisfaction dropped during their first year but then remained stable.

At two months, the stayers and leavers had just about the same frequencies of social contacts with both veteran and new American migrants. Then over the next three years, stayers showed a small increase in their contacts with veteran Americans, but had a clear drop in contacts with new American migrants. Similarly, their contacts with non-American new migrants showed a substantial drop.

The major differences between stayers and leavers occurred at the level of perceptions. Stayers were twice as likely as leavers to be "quite sure" of staying in Israel and two to three times as likely to feel "fully" like an Israeli. These feelings of the stayers remained pretty stable over the three panel years.

[1] The 37% leaving and 63% staying at least three years are weighted figures with the weighting process deriving from the disproportionality characteristics of the sample design of the Immigrant Absorption Survey. The end of the third panel year actually covers the years 1972–1974.

Table 6.2. Characteristics of Migrants (Stayers and Leavers)
at Varying Stages of the Adjustment-Absorption Process (in Percent)

	Leavers—2 months		Stayers (in Israel)		
Characteristics	In Israel	2 months	1 year	2 years	3 years
Satisfactions					
Economically quite satisfied	33	40	33	32	34
Socially well satisfied	31	35	35	32	36
Well satisfied with housing	46	48	43	46	47
Quite satisfied with Hebrew progress	27	30	39	41	42
Contacts					
Frequent social contacts with veteran					
Americans	19	18	28	23	22
Frequent social contacts with new					
American migrants	46	45	42	42	38
Frequent social contacts with new					
non-American migrants	34	30	20	21	15
Perceptions					
Feeling fully like an Israeli	7	16	17	16	20
Probability of staying: Quite sure	25	52	51	52	50

SOURCE: Dashefsky and Lazerwitz (1986).

These findings suggest that the stayers and leavers arrive with different initial attitudes toward their new experiences. Those who are more confident of staying are, in fact, more likely to stay and to feel like Israelis, develop satisfactions with their new lives, and reduce contacts with other migrants who may reinforce nonadaptive orientations.[2]

Those who stayed differed from those who left on religious items as well. Consistently, those who stayed were more religious, that is, more likely to attend synagogue services weekly (36% vs. 20%), to have fasted on their last Yom Kippur abroad (68% vs. 47%), or to prefer the Orthodox Jewish denomination (35% vs. 19%), and had more Jewish education (32% Jewish day schools) in contrast to 24% of those who left.[3] Again, following these percentages, we might well conclude that religion and Jewish education, which so strongly separated these migrants from their American source population, were also important factors in their absorption process.

Yet, bivariate percentage tables in themselves do not permit solid conclusions. Rather, religion ought to be forced to compete with other factors in a

[2]Derived from Dashefsky and Lazerwitz (1986, p. 50).
[3]Derived from Dashefsky and Lazerwitz (1983, p. 268).

Table 6.3. Major Factors Distinguishing between Those Who Stay
or Leave and Amount of AID Variance Explained (Israel Immigrant
Absorption Survey, First and Second Panel Waves in Percent)

	Amount of AID variance explained	
Major factors	First wave	Second wave
Confidence of staying	12	14
Able to speak Hebrew prior to migration	3	1
Member of Jewish organizations before migration	2	—
Fewer social contacts with new arrivals from countries other than in North America	1	2
Marital status	1	—
Sex	2	—
Less frequent synagogue attendance abroad	1	—
Preferred a denomination versus not preferring one	1	—
Age	1	1
Social contacts with veteran settlers from North America	—	1
Total AID variance explained	24	19

SOURCE: Dashefsky and Lazerwitz (1983).

regression model. Enough research has been done with multiple regression models of Jewish identification derived from the National Jewish Population Survey data to indicate that it is highly likely that religion strongly differentiates between these Jewish migrants to Israel and the adults of the entire American Jewish community (Lazerwitz and Harrison, 1980). What then can be said about the "staying-leaving" differentiation? An excellent method for determining the factors that indicate the maximum differences between those who stay or leave is the automatic interaction detection system (AID) described in Sonquist, Baker, and Morgan (1971).[4]

The automatic interaction detection system is used in Table 6.3 to determine the set of survey variables that differentiate between those who stayed throughout the three panel years and those who left during this time. Inspection of the data indicates that only a minor portion of the variance resulting from survey respondents actually staying or leaving Israel can be explained. Just 24% of the differ-

[4]This technique is a variety of model II analysis of variance. It works by successive analysis of variance applications and requires a dependent variable that is either an interval scale or a 0, 1 two-category split. The independent variables can be either ordinal or nominal scale ones. When done, this method tells how much dependent variable variance can be explained by the dominating independent variables. Another advantage of AID is that it does not assume an additive model and can indicate the presence of any major variable interactions.

ence between stayers and leavers can be explained by the first survey wave variables and even less, 19%, by second survey wave variables.

The one factor that is relatively effective in distinguishing those who stay from those who leave is the persistently greater confidence of remaining in Israel expressed by those who do actually stay (12% of variance in the first wave). Beyond this variable, ability to speak Hebrew before migration accounts for 3% of the variance, greater involvement in Jewish organizations before migrating accounts for 2%, as does gender (with women more likely to stay than men). After this there are a series of quite minor factors, each of which explains 1% of the variance. They indicate that being married, having less frequent contact with new arrivals who are not from North America, less frequent synagogue attendance abroad, having a denominational preference, being 30 years of age or older, and more frequent contacts with veteran North American settlers are all associated with staying.

In a multifactor approach, then, the religious difference between stayers and leavers is not nearly as important as other variables. The limits of secondary analysis take over at this point, in that the available survey data do not explore why respondents feel more or less confident about staying in Israel. The additional 5% of variance explained deriving from Hebrew language ability and involvement in Jewish organizations does give some weight to Jewish education and ethnic communal activity. Neither, though, are religious variables.

After doing the AID analysis, 19 survey variables for the same first and second panel waves were again used to differentiate between stayers and leavers. This time analysis was done with a dummy variable multiple regression technique especially designed for nominal or ordinal dependent variables. This technique is the multivariate nominal scale analysis (MNA) technique described in Andrews and Messenger (1973).[5]

The results of this predictive endeavor are shown in Table 6.4 for both the first and second panel interviewing waves. The table shows that applying MNA to the data of the Immigrant Absorption Survey readily predicts those who stay. However, the survey's data fail to predict, readily, those who leave. At the first wave, 31% of the leavers were predicted as staying; at the second wave, 52% of those yet destined to leave Israel were predicted as staying. Overall, about 15% of the survey's respondents at the two panel waves belong to sort of a "swing category" of people who, on interviewing, would appear to be among those who will be staying, but who do leave.

This MNA analysis effort does suggest a figure that captures the various migration and absorption factors. First, in Figure 6.1 there are a set of demographic variables that are directly associated with staying in or leaving Israel, such as being over 30, female, or married. Second, there are a group of variables

[5]Adapted from Dashefsky and Lazerwitz (1983, pp. 268–270).

Table 6.4. MNA Predictions on Staying or Leaving
and Actual Results (Immigrant Absorption Survey,
First and Second Panel Waves in Percent)

| | Predicted outcome | | |
Actual outcome	Leave	Stay	Base
First wave			
Leave	69	31	100
Stay	15	85	100
Second wave			
Leave	48	52	100
Stay	7	93	100

SOURCE: Dashefsky and Lazerwitz (1986).

that reflect background factors in the American Jewish community that existed prior to migration, such as activity in Jewish organizations and ability to speak Hebrew before coming to Israel. A third set of variables that emerge out of absorption experiences in Israel are also apparent. Foremost among these are contacts with veteran settlers and satisfactions with the basic areas of daily life in

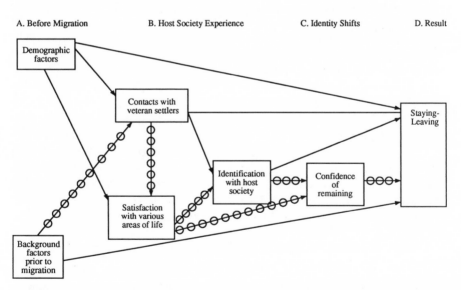

Figure 6.1. A model of American migration. SOURCE: Adapted from Dashefsky and Lazerwitz (1986).

Israel, such as jobs, housing, and social life. These absorption experience variables, in their turn, seem to build the identification with Israel and Israelis and with the important factor of confidence of remaining. Through such confidence, these variables operate indirectly upon "staying-leaving." (In the model, arrows with circles represent the stronger factors.[6])

These statistics indicate that initially what really counts are the set of background factors carried by the migrants. For example, the first panel wave of American emigrants in Israel not only measures the beginning of the absorption process, it also represents the end of the process that led to the migration decision. North American emigrants are quite different from the vast majority of North Americans. For example, in the case of Olim, the strong Jewish religious and education factors that separate these respondents from their fellow Jews in North America play a fairly minor role in absorption success. Prior Jewish religious involvement can move a person to Israel, but it will not necessarily keep a person there. By the time of the second survey panel wave, the Israeli experience takes over as the effective determinant of migration success.[7]

In a study of Italian immigrants in Australia, Heiss (1969) discovered the complexity of trying to sort out the process by which premigration traits relate to later assimilation. We have tried, however, to show the nature of these complex associations that follow a path from motivations for migration, adjustments in the adopted country, and the factors in remaining or returning to the home country based on the Israeli data. As with Heiss's Australian data, we do not have the complete explanation we would like because our data from the Australian group do not permit construction of a path model based on those who actually stayed compared to those who actually left. Nevertheless, we are able to make some similar comparisons for the emigrants in Australia based on the distinction between those who thought at the time of the interview they would stay more than five years, whom we also designated as "stayers," and those who thought they would leave within five years, whom we designated as "leavers." These groups differ from those we called settlers and sojourners, a distinction based on their initial intentions.

In examining the various blocks of variables described in Figure 6.1, we find with respect to demographic factors that stayers were more likely to be married on arrival than leavers (58% vs. 49%). Furthermore, stayers were more likely to be married to an Australian on arrival than leavers (23% vs. 11%) and less likely to be college educated or professionally trained than leavers (38% vs. 64%).

With respect to background factors before migration, stayers were more

---

[6]Scott and Scott (1989, p. 20) present a similar model as the guiding scheme for their research on the adaptation of Australian immigrants.
[7]Adapted from Dashefsky and Lazerwitz (1986, pp. 51–59).

likely to have made prior visits to Australia, to have low levels of home owner-ship in the United States, and/or a minimum of other social ties to the States to force their return. Indeed, few owned any assets at all; 95% of all respondents claimed they did not even own a car in the United States before they relocated to Australia.

In examining the migration experience of the Australian group, we found that stayers were more likely than leavers to claim strong ties to family including spouse or children (39% vs. 19%), to relatives other than spouse or children in Australia (22% vs. 17%), to Australian spouses (48% vs. 4% of leavers), to other social relationships in Australia (70% vs. 36%), to three or more good Australian friends (88% vs. 66%), and to occupation in Australia (47% vs. 26%). However, stayers and leavers are equally as likely to claim they are satisfied with their Australian jobs (60% of stayers vs. 61% of leavers). Furthermore, stayers experi-enced relatively modest adjustments. Only 26% of stayers stated they had to make three or more significant adjustments versus 36% of leavers. Moreover, stayers reported that their social life was better in Australia (29% vs. 13%) and that as compared to leavers their leisure life was better in Australia than the United States (28% vs. 21%). In addition, stayers as compared to leavers felt more Australian than American (27% vs. 4%), and thought they belonged more in Australia than America (59% vs. 21%). In fact, 32% of the leavers felt uncomfortable or out of place in Australia versus 8% of stayers. Finally, stayers in comparison to leavers felt stronger political ties to Australia (29% vs. 13%) and believed that their Australian standard of living was the same or better than in America (75% vs. 62%).

With regard to contacts with veteran settlers in Australia, we found an individualistic pattern of spatial and social assimilation. A substantial proportion (46%) had no good American friends in Australia. The absence of a language barrier in Australia made this a significant contrast to Israeli society, where language among other factors created an Anglo-Saxon culture. Furthermore, there was a high likelihood of marriage to an Australian while in Australia and a weakening of social ties to people in the States (especially friends, but also family). Only parents were perceived as significant family for migrants as ex-tended family ties were also weakened.

In considering shifts in identity and identification with their host society, 60% of respondents felt "very Australian" or felt "as much Australian as Ameri-can" and 88% felt as comfortable or more comfortable in Australia than in the States. Furthermore, of those who originally intended to return to the States within five years, 35% now intended definitely to settle, 36% were undecided, and only 25% intended to return to the United States within five years. Of those who were originally undecided about staying, 40% definitely intended to settle and 52% were undecided. Of those who arrived intending to settle, 72% still intended definitely to settle and 18% were undecided. Respondents who most likely stated their intention to return to the United States within five years were either unmarried, married to an American, had weak Australian friendships, had strong social ties to the United States, weak occupational ties to Australia, or simply originally intended to return in five years. This latter point represents the obverse of the data on Olim, for whom those who had the greatest confidence in staying actually remained in Israel.

YANKS AND OLIM: SIMILARITIES AND DIFFERENCES

Much effort has been spent thus far in gaining an understanding of these two migrating streams of Americans—one to Australia and one to Israel. They have at least one major characteristic in common. They both are Americans reacting to less developed countries. By examining the way they react, we can learn something about Americans.

For example, both groups of migrants complained about having to adjust to a lower standard of living. Those going to Israel, for the most part, expected a lower standard of living. Those going to Australia were not always aware of this fact and had to endure it subsequent to their arrival in Australia. Both groups found it difficult to accept their lower living standards and expectations. In other words, Americans moving abroad face an inevitable struggle to deal with a lower standard of living and find it hard to do this. While the very high U.S. standard of living makes it difficult for Americans to live abroad, remarkably over the long haul about one quarter going to Australia and one half going to Israel endure the adjustments (see Chapter 7).

Both groups, however, constantly complained about the lower standards of work efficiency and work quality they found in Israel or in Australia. The "Puritan work ethic" has become a part of the "American way of life," and its internalized components go abroad with Americans. It shapes how they view the new world surrounding them.

In addition, both groups of Americans, for the most part, had been fairly successful in the United States. The members of both migrating groups had, typically, achieved a high level of education. The members of both groups, through their education success and through their high occupational and standard of living expectations showed themselves to be hardworking, competitive people with high personal standards. They were, and are, bearers of the admirable traits in the American cultural tradition.

As such culture bearers, they thought the different societies they moved into ought to aspire to their high achievement and productivity standards. When such societies responded with their own "lower" standards, these migrating Americans were disappointed and forced to adjust by lowering their expectations of the "new world" surrounding them.

Over time, many of the American emigrants have reacted to these difficulties by going back to the United States. Those who stay try to maintain their standards and do their best to promote them in their new surroundings. In turn, their propensity to work hard and to achieve high standards serve to promote them more rapidly in their new work environments.

For example, in Israel, Americans are disproportionately associated with organizations concerned about civil rights and civil liberties or with the "quality of the environment." In turn, such "American interests" in Israel have served to attract those Israelis who are also concerned about the same issues. As a result, such issues serve as a bridge between those members of Israeli society and the American Olim.

Gitelman (1982) has contrasted the adjustments of American and Soviet migrants to Israel. He describes American migrants to Israel as complaining about the lack of efficiency of the Israeli governmental bureaucracy in terms similar to what we have quoted Americans in Australia saying about their experiences with the Australian bureaucracy. Gitelman's Americans complained that "officials did not have a book of rules and procedures available when dealing with their clients. . . . Explanations were not given as to why petitions were rejected" (1982, p. 49). Gitelman concludes that "professionals (Americans) often find Israeli practices and procedures in their fields to be archaic, inefficient, and unreasonable" (1982, p. 133).

Again, Americans in Israel, like Americans in Australia, retain pride in their American backgrounds, an ongoing interest in American affairs, and do not give up their United States citizenship. Unlike Australian law, Israeli law permits, indeed facilitates, the acquisition of dual nationality. After three years in Israel, with the possibility of extending it to four years, Jews who request visa extensions as permanent residents are just given Israeli citizenship. No legal act is required by them nor is any oath taken. It is the government of Israel which, in effect, tells immigrants that from now on it will regard them as Israeli citizens. Since this process does not conflict with United States law, the American immigrant to Israel winds up with citizenship in both Israel and the United States. (However, those who so wish may opt out of this automatic citizenship by stating that they do not wish to become citizens.)

Gitelman points out that Americans in Israel have a positive view of the United States. "Even those who said they came to Israel in order to escape negative aspects of American life remain interested in American affairs and were anxious to see the United States solve its problems" (1982, p. 207). He refers to Americans in Israel feeling that what Israel could learn from the United States was efficiency, civility, tolerance, and politeness (Gitelman, 1982, p. 216).

Similarly, Berman reports finding the same reactions in his study of American Olim. He quotes them as saying, "conditions of work, particularly the level of efficiency, represent a problem for many respondents in their present work" (1978, p. 60).

Antonovsky and Katz (1979) also report that their respondents, American migrants to Israel during the 1960s, strongly complained about the lack of efficiency at work, in shops, or with the governmental bureaucracy. Again, a repetition of the same theme was found among American migrants to Australia.

The considerable similarity of the "American background" viewpoint shows up again when we examine the number of annual migrants to either Australia or Israel. Both streams peaked during the 1970–1972 period. These peaks represent a response to the turbulence running through American life in this Vietnam War period and the attractive economic and social conditions prevailing in the two receiving societies.

However, there are two striking dissimilarities between these two groups of migrants. While it is an ideological commitment that is important in moving most Americans to Israel, ideology plays little, if any, role in moving Americans to Australia. Moreover, 60% of the migrants to Israel are women while 60% of those going to Australia are men.

Compared to the U.S. population as a whole, both groups of migrants are disproportionately young with 42% of the migrants to Israel being from 18 to 29 years of age and 42% of the migrants to Australia being from 20 to 29 years of age. Again, both groups are well educated with 42% of the migrants to Israel having a college degree or better and 37% of the migrants to Australia having a college degree or better. Both groups also have high-status occupations with 40% of the migrants to Israel having held professional jobs in the United States and 45% of the migrants to Australia working in Australian professional jobs.

With such educational and occupational backgrounds, it is not surprising that both groups of migrants joined the middle and upper middle classes of their new societies. Unlike the historic international migrant who began life in a "new world" on the bottom of its socioeconomic system, both groups of migrants went right into middle-class status and life.

Their marital statuses are similar with just about 40% of both groups of migrants being single upon arrival in their new countries. (Unlike the Australian data, the Israeli marital data do not permit separating migrant marriages into those with Israelis and those with fellow Americans.)

SUMMARY[8]

The analysis of emigrants to Israel suggests that first there are a set of demographic factors that affect absorption, such as being over 30, female, and married. Second, there are factors related to the experiences in the United States prior to emigration, such as involvement in Jewish organizations and the ability to speak Hebrew before coming to Israel. Third, there are variables that directly

[8]Adapted in part from Dashefsky, DeAmicis, and Lazerwitz (1984, pp. 341–342).

relate to the experience abroad, such as contacts with veteran settlers and satis-factions with various basic areas of daily life—jobs, housing, and social life in Israel. All of these experiences lead to the centrally most important variable affecting absorption—"confidence of remaining"—which explained 12% of the variance or half of all the variance we could explain (24%).

In the case of American migrants to Australia, those whom we labeled permanent settlers arrived fully intending to stay. About a third of the inter-viewed respondents and 35% of the other survey respondents definitely intended to settle in Australia at the time of their arrival. Often settlement intentions were linked to such family ties as marriage to an Australian. Nearly half of the settlers claimed that family ties in Australia were important as a reason for choosing to go there. Another important explanation for deciding to settle was to pursue entrepreneurial or other occupational opportunities. Finally, some were escaping personal and (less often) social problems back in America. (Yes, there are some alienated Americans in Australia.)

In the case of Americans in Israel, the proportion who perceived themselves as staying was slightly higher. Of all those interviewed in the Israeli panel survey two months after their arrival, 41% stated that the probability of their staying was "quite sure." After three years, 63% of the original sample were still actually living in Israel.

In addition to the permanent settlers in Australia, there were the sojourners who went to Australia with vaguely formed intentions of eventually returning to America. They went as adventurers, wanderers, casual job seekers, or as visi-tors. Sojourners were generally younger than settlers. They were in a crease in their life cycle. They had been freed from adolescent restraints. They were uncommitted to career or home ownership. In addition, they had been culturally encouraged to travel and to seek their fortunes. For all of these reasons, they were free to go abroad before taking up the serious commitments of adult life in America.

The comparisons of intended settlers and intended sojourners among Ameri-can emigrants in Australia is strikingly similar to the comparison of actual stayers and leavers among American emigrants in Israel. This latter comparison shows that the leavers were younger and more likely to be single and male. The leavers were somewhat more likely to be professionals and slightly more likely to be college graduates than the stayers. All of these characteristics made it possible for them to return. The ones who remained were likely to be those with a greater intention to remain and greater confidence in staying and who subsequently increased their social contacts and interaction with the host community. The two groups of emigrants, nevertheless, differed in two areas: ideology and gender. Those migrating to Israel were more ideologically motivated whereas those going to Australia were not. Furthermore, a majority of emigrants moving to Israel were female whereas the inverse was true for Australia.

7

Retention or Reemigration
Why They Remain or Return[1]

One of our Australian respondents, when pressed by the interviewer about the decision to remain or return to America, replied:

> Mainly we talk about it (returning) when people ask us about it. It isn't something that comes up once a week or even once a month. Once a month would be generous. . . . No, it sort of happened (remaining), I think. I mean, we don't know if the right job came up or something happened, but we talk less about whether or not we'll go back to the States, but more about where we'd like to move in Australia.

Just as the topic of emigration is a less popular one for study than immigration, so, too, is the subject of return migration less likely to be studied than the motivation for migration. To be sure, there is some research on return migration for English migrants to Australia (Appleyard, 1962), Western migrants to their countries of origin from Israel (Blejer and Goldberg, 1980), Italian migrants to the United States (Cerase, 1967), Canadian migrants to the United States (Comay, 1971), returning Israelis (Elizur, 1974, 1979), Danish migrants to America (Hvidt, 1975), British migrants to Canada (Richmond, 1968), and intra-European return migration (Rose, 1969). These studies suggest that the major factors in such returns are lower than expected financial gains, family and friendship ties to be restored by returning, and, for Israelis, patriotic feelings about one's homeland.

Americans in Australia and Israel are more likely to return to their native land than virtually any other migrant group. The return migration rate is variously estimated as 28% (Australian Department of Labour and Immigration, 1973), 72% (Australian Immigration Advisory Council Committee on Social

---

[1]Parts of this chapter are adapted and expanded from Dashefsky and Lazerwitz (1983, pp. 271–273; 1986, pp. 58–59).

Patterns, 1973), and 45% (Finifter and Finifter, 1980a). Regardless of the estimate, the reemigration rate for Americans is high.

Much of this variation is dependent on the time period over which the rate of remaining or returning is calculated. Obviously the longer the period of time measured, the higher the return rate as can be seen in our data for Israel. For the three-year period 1969–1972, the return migration rate was 37%, but for the period 1961–1972 the rate was 58%. The difference between the migrants to Israel and Australia is that the former intend to stay, unless they decide to leave, while the latter intend to leave unless they decide to stay.

RETURN MIGRATION

The gathering body of research on emigrating Americans largely ignores the question of why so many return to America. The methodological problems of such research are very considerable. For instance, how can Americans who are definitely returning to the United States be identified and questioned? How can Americans who have gone home be located for interviews?

While we were successful in locating a small sample of emigrants who returned to the United States, we also interviewed and surveyed a number of people who were convinced they would return to America, although we do not know if any actually went back. Such plans were highly elastic and easily deferrable. We found that those who intended to return were mostly those whose initial intentions were to stay for one or two years. Perhaps they had a short-term contract with their employer; or perhaps they felt it was time to return to America and take up life-as-normal; or perhaps some were disappointed with the life they found in Australia or Israel, including some Americans who went intending to settle.

The only other published research addressing this question for Yanks is the Australian Department of Labour and Immigration Study (1969, 1971). The follow-up on the initial survey concluded that Americans departed for the following reasons: (1) "Working tourists": more than half the departees had come for "travel and adventure." (2) Most departees had lower-status occupations than nondepartees, limited prospects, and low earning power, especially clerks, tradespersons, and semiskilled workers. Finifter and Finifter (1980a) reported that many of their respondents, especially those they termed "new settlers," intended to leave, but they did not speculate as to their reasons.

With respect to returned Olim, the literature is a little larger. Engel (1970) found for a sample of 256 returned Olim that "job opportunities, housing, and cost of living were practical considerations for leaving. The desire to live in a Jewish state, experience a religious environment, and enjoy a cultural life were ideological motives for staying" (1970, p. 183). Engel's study was based on self-administered questionnaires completed by individuals who lived in Israel for at least one year prior to 1967. A more recent study was conducted by Waxman and Appel (1986, p. 21), who interviewed a "snowball" sample of 71 returned Olim who had emigrated in 1967 or later and remained at least one year. Waxman and Appel caution that their survey "provides no clear insights concerning their reasons for going and coming," but conclude that "the reasons they gave for returning to the United States were primarily economic and familial, exacerbated by what they perceived as a lack of professional opportunities, difficulties of daily life and estrangement from certain aspects of Israeli society" (1986, p. 21).

It is somewhat tautological to argue that those whose adjustment problems were most severe were those most likely to return. Instead, since we interpret a significant portion of American settlement in Australia as an emergent process, rather than a predetermined decision, it follows that the bulk of returnees were essentially complying with their original intentions. By either resisting the enticements of Australian life, or reacting to differences in culture and living standards, or rejecting Australian values and norms, many Americans never found a reason to modify original plans to return home. Returning was as unheroic as going in the first place.

It is possible to obtain a good estimate of the percentage of our migrant streams that remain in the two host countries by starting with an early census report on the number of American permanent residents. Then to this figure one adds governmental reports on the number of American residents arriving from one census to the next. Finally, one divides this "expected" estimate, if no one left, by the number of American residents reported by the next census. (Of course, this method ignores American deaths; given that these Americans were so young, deaths were likely very few and ignored.) Table 7.1 presents the findings of our cumulative review of rates of remaining and returning for the Yanks and Olim.

The *remain* percentage for Yanks dropped from the first census period onward throughout the approximately 20 years under review. Note that the decrease was substantial for Yanks from 1961 to 1970 (48%) and for 1961 to 1975 (30%). Hence, the return rate appeared to slow down for the 1975–1981 period. (The staying rates for both settlers and sojourners were quite similar.) Over a period of 20 years, 25% of American migrants to Australia appeared to have remained.[2]

For American Olim going to Israel, an opposite pattern appears. The initial 11-year remain rate was 42%. However, during the second part of the approximately 20-year period, it improved so that the overall percentage remaining increased to 48%. The three-year staying rate was 63% for the migrants of the panel survey years of 1969 to 1971.

[2]This is in contrast to an 80% staying rate for all immigrants to Australia according to Lukomskyj and Richards (1986).

Table 7.1. Rates of Remaining and Returning
(in Percent)
for American Migrants to Australia
(Yanks) and Israel (Olim)

Time period	Remain	Return
Yanks		
1961–1970	48	52
1961–1975	30	70
1961–1981	25	75
Olim		
1961–1972	42	58
1969–1971[a]	63	37
1961–1983	48	52

[a]Migrant three-year panel survey (to 1974). See discussion
of Israel Immigrant Absorption Survey in Chapter 2.
SOURCE: Australian Censuses of 1961, 1970, 1975, and
1981 and Israeli Censuses of 1961, 1972, and
1983.

Thus, the Americans in Australia began with a somewhat better remain rate of 48% against the Americans in Israel rate of 42%. However, the staying rate in Australia showed a steady drop over the approximate 20 years being observed while the staying rate in Israel improved. By the time of the most recent censuses in both countries, the overall remain rate for Israel was (48%), just about twice that of the Australian rate (25%).[3]

Since both groups originated from the same host society and were very similar in their sociodemographic profile, the difference in their staying rate was more a function of their social psychological characteristics or responses of the host society. While for both groups self-expressive motivations for migration predominated, those emigrants in Australia had more personal (or "egoistic" in the Durkheimian sense) motives while those in Israel had more collectivistic (or "altruistic" in the Durkheimian sense) and ideological ones. Perhaps this latter type of motivation, coupled with the response of the host society, produced a greater staying rate.

Rarely does one research project study all of the phenomena we do consider, including motivations for migration, the problems of adjustment, and the factors in return migration and reintegration. We were successful, however, in obtaining a small "snowball" sample ($n = 46$) of returned migrants and interviewed them in the United States subsequent to their return.

[3]Scott and Scott (1989, pp. 24–25) also discussed the return rate of European migrants to Australia, which was considerably lower than for Americans.

We sought to distinguish these "returnees" from those potential migrants planning to live in Israel, or "premigrants," and those Olim living in Israel. Were they very much different from those in the other phases of the migration cycle? Did they resemble the larger American Jewish population or were they more similar to other migrants or potential migrants?

The returnees included a percentage of younger adults (31%) very much like the premigrants (34%) and more similar to the Olim (42%) than American Jews in general (21%). Similarly, 39% of the returnees were unmarried as were 40% of the Olim. At this time American Jews were 20% unmarried. In terms of gender a disproportionate number of the returnees were women (65%). Slightly more women were premigrants (54%) and Olim (57%) in comparison to American Jews in general (52%). With respect to generation, the returnees were distinguished in having such a small proportion in the first generation (11%) and such a high proportion of third or more generation individuals (57%) compared to Olim (40%), premigrants (29%), or American Jews (20%).

Among the returnees, 58% reported they had children ($n = 45$) compared to slightly less than the 66% of the premigrants ($n = 35$). In contrast to the premigrants, in which nearly one sixth of them had children living in Israel, *none* of the returnees had any children living in Israel. This is a further indication that family ties play a role in migration to Israel or return to the United States.

Thus, with respect to such biosocial background characteristics as age and marital status, the returnees resembled the premigrants and Olim in contrast to American Jews as a whole. In terms of generational status, the returnees were exceptional in that they were disproportionately third generation like the premigrants and Olim, only more so.

One tentative conclusion from this limited sample is that the returnees resembled more the premigrants and Olim than American Jews in general with respect to the biosocial background characteristics of age and marital status. With respect to gender differences and generational status, the similarity with the premigrants and Olim is even greater. Thus, the conditions of youth and singleness that freed Americans to emigrate to Israel also freed them to return. Add to this the absence of any family ties in Israel, and the picture that the biosocial characteristics described for the returnees is one of a lack of attributes that make for social integration.

In the area of socioeconomic status, the returnees, like the premigrants, were more highly educated than American Jews in general, only more so. Eighty-three percent of the returnees had a college degree in comparison to 46% of the premigrants, 42% of the Olim, and only 33% of American Jews. Moreover, in terms of occupational distribution, 61% of the returnees were engaged in professional work (mostly teaching and social service) compared to 40% of Olim and 29% both for the premigrants and American Jews as a whole.

Here again, the returnees possessed more of the characteristics of the premigrants and Olim than American Jews. High education levels and having a professional occupation may make it extremely difficult for returnees to successfully integrate themselves into Israeli society. They may not be able to achieve the levels of professional and intellectual challenge in Israel that they found in the United States.

There are at least three aspects to the patterns of Jewish identification where comparisons among the groups are possible. First, there is the intensity of Jewish education, which was measured by the percent in each sample that received a day school education. For the returnees, 50% had received at least seven hours of instruction per week of Jewish education. This may be seen as an approximate equivalent of day school education, which 25% of the premigrants and 29% of Olim had received compared to only 4% of American Jews as a whole (as reported in the 1971 National Jewish Population Survey).

A second area where comparisons can be made is that of synagogue attendance. For returnees, 30% attended synagogue services at least weekly before emigration. This compared with 37% of the premigrants and 29% of Olim who attended services at least weekly before migration while only 8% of American Jews attended that frequently (in the 1971 survey).

Finally, with respect to the Jewish identification pattern, we found that 86% of the returnees spoke some Hebrew. This proportion was understandably higher than that for the premigrants (64%) and for Olim (70%) who spoke some Hebrew after two months in Israel. This rather high percentage, of course, is not surprising given that the returnees had lived in Israel. No comparable data are available for the American Jewish population, but clearly the knowledge of spoken Hebrew must be substantially lower than for the above groups given the small percentage of American Jewish day school graduates.

In sum, these three dimensions of Jewish identification indicate that the returnees were no less Jewishly identified than the premigrants and Olim. One cannot argue that the former returned because they did not have a strong enough Jewish identification or because they knew no Hebrew.

Indeed, Engel (1970), who studied a group of returned migrants who had lived in Israel prior to 1967, reported that Jewish identification, an expressive issue, was a motive for staying whereas instrumental reasons, such as job and housing concerns, were factors in returning.

CROSS-PRESSURES OF REMAINING OR RETURNING IN FOUR QUADRANTS

Tables 2.3 and 3.2 on motivations were formulated as a result of initially examining the perceived factors in return migration for a sample of Americans who had lived in Israel ($n = 46$). Among those items most frequently cited by the respondents were such others-expressive dimensions as familial reunification and adjustment. For example, the factor most commonly mentioned by the returnees from Israel to America as contributing "a lot" (as opposed to "somewhat," "little," or "none") was reunification with the family in America. Indeed, 65% of the sample offered this as a major reason for returning, and 52% said problems of family adjustment in Israel were reasons for returning. The median score for this category was 58%. At a second level of concern were such self-instrumental factors as the frustrations related to dealing with the bureaucracy (52% thought it a major contributing factor in returning), job (46%), daily living (46%), and housing (30%). The median score for this category was 46%. At the next lower level of intensity were self-expressive concerns such as the personal lack of a sense of community (42%), cultural difficulties such as language problems (28%), or concerns about Jewish life (20%). The median score for this category was 28%. At the lowest level of concern were issues of an others-instrumental type such as government politics (13%) or military service (9%). The median score in this category was 11%. We could find, however, no respondents who elaborated on these matters. Hence, we report no data for this quadrant. Perhaps they were more important as an underlying issue, but we could not confirm this notion. Waxman (1989, p. 178), who relied on our categorization to study the factors in return migration, found similar ordering of responses based on an independently gathered sample of 71 returnees. Thus, the same rank ordering of categories prevailed in accounting for return migration with the greatest proportion explaining their return on the basis of familial factors (others-expressive)

Table 7.2. Cross-Pressures of Remaining or Returning

Locus of concern	Cross-pressures (remain vs. return)	
	Expressive	Instrumental
Self	Political concerns Sense of community Cultural differences	Occupation Bureaucracy Housing Daily living
	A	B
	C	D
Others	Marriage Familial reunification and harmony Education of children	Military service

followed by the other categories listed above. This fits in with the discussion at the end of Chapter 4 indicating the ambivalence of parents about their offspring's emigration to Israel.

Table 7.2 captures the major considerations that emigrants to Australia and Israel grappled with in assessing whether to remain in their adopted land or return to their native land. It does not exhaust all of the possibilities but reflects the ones in our data.

It will be recalled that in assessing the motives for migration, we began with "self-expressive" concerns in quadrant A. In examining the problems in adjustment, the most salient were in quadrant B, "self-instrumental" issues. Now in analyzing the migrants' decision to remain or return, the most salient were in quadrant C, "others-expressive." That is where we shall begin.

MARRIAGE, FAMILY, AND CHILDREN (QUADRANT C)

For many Americans, marriage to an Australian was reason enough to go there in the first place. Moreover, migrants with Australian spouses were more likely to go as settlers rather than sojourners. Marriage to an Australian in Australia also created a strong bond to the country, perhaps the single most important step an American could make in the direction of settlement.

More than two thirds (69%) of all those married to Australians also intended to remain in Australia for good. About one third of unmarried Americans (32%) were much less likely to intend to settle and about another third (30%) were much more likely to think they would return to the States within five years. The relationship between marital status and intentions to settle remained basically unchanged regardless of length of residence.

The simple fact of marriage to an Australian did not necessarily indicate an intention to remain, but the association appears very strong. About 30% of all who arrived unmarried were now married to Australians, and all of them intended to settle. Conversely, of those who were single on arrival and who expected to return within five years, none was married to an Australian.

Such marriages had consequences that many could not anticipate in terms of settlement. It brought pressures for expanded living space, more secure employment, larger income, and changes in daily routines (shopping, eating, recreation, and so on). Moreover, it usually added to the Yank's social circle a whole array of new relationships, primarily in-laws and the spouse's friendship networks. Daily routines had to be reordered to fit new responsibilities, and the spouse's relationships were all in Australia, and usually nearby. The American may not have valued these new relationships at first, but the Australian certainly did. Thus, rather than the Australians being drawn out of their social network, the Americans were likely to be drawn into them (unless, of course, they left the country).

The American now had a *spouse* who might be reluctant to abandon these people, if given a choice.

"If given a choice" meant different things to men and women. Women usually expected no such choice, but men who expected to return to the United States could often be persuaded or constrained to defer their expected return without necessarily revising their settlement intentions. This is what happened to Duane, who first visited Australia with the U.S. Navy:

> I was in the U.S. Navy, on a cruiser, the Helena, and in those days the U.S. fleet used to arrive every May to commemorate the Battle of the Coral Sea. At the time the ship was in Melbourne, I met my wife at the Australian-American Association, at a cocktail party. I was here 10 days. Eventually I went back to the States and we began to correspond with each other. I came out the following March, ten months later. I came out on my own. I had finished up my hitch with the Navy, and I just grabbed a plane and came on back to sort of go around the world and use Melbourne as the first step. Sort of never made it back.

The interviewer asked, "You came out with the intention of staying for awhile and moving on?"

> Just moving on, I guess. We became engaged. We were still going to go back. We were going to be married, honeymoon on the boat trip going back. But 3 weeks prior to the wedding I had an auto accident. Hurt my knee pretty badly, and decided we'd better stay and see it through. By the time it came to court, it was 2 years later and two children later, and we said, "Well, looking ahead, we'll just sort of stay."

The interviewer continued, "You make it sound like you were simply putting off until later the decision to go back. The decision wasn't to stay, but to stay for awhile."

> Right, yah, for awhile. And what happened was we came back from our honeymoon, two weeks home and found out Jackie was pregnant . . . and that was it. Three in three years. Then there were other factors that did definitely sort of hold us back, namely you just don't pack off a couple of youngsters and go back. That's when we started collecting furniture and things like that. Every day we stayed it was that much harder to make the break, I guess.

It was clear that marrying Jackie was the beginning of a dramatic new phase in Duane's life: in-laws, career, children, serious consideration of the quality of life virtues of Australia, questions about what life might be like for raising a family in America, and no real reason to return.

Events and decisions attendant to marriage to an Australian might be evaluated in terms of immediate life-situations in Australia rather than with a view toward settlement or return to America: the short-run outlook overshadows the long-run perspective. Terry, for instance, lived in America for 20 years with his Australian wife Joan before moving to Melbourne, to live on his retirement income. They could not really think of leaving largely because of her (that is, their) family responsibilities.

"Think there's any chance you'll go back?" asked the interviewer.

> Well, you know . . . the longer you stay somewhere, then you start to accumulate problems. I have our little niece and her mother here, broken family, now they've been with us for about 7 years. Then the mother-in-law, she's 83 years old, we have her down here for months. These things, if you didn't have them you don't know that you might be quicker to do something.

Marrying an Australian changed the migrant's status from outsider to insider more quickly than might have happened otherwise. But such marriages did not necessarily lead to changes in migrants' self-perceptions, from feeling that they were Americans to feeling they were Australians. This was more an outcome of many years of living there regardless of marital status. But they were likely to feel more comfortable living in Australia than in America, compared to those who were single or married to Americans.

As with marriage, the arrival of children was in itself a commitment, as well as the immediate context for subsequent commitments in other areas of life. The mere presence of children did not constitute a pressure to settle, for after all many Americans had moved with families that included one or more children. While children did not pose an extraordinary restriction on travel, the birth of children could produce a profound change in the Yank's immediate and relatively unencumbered circumstances. As a parent, he or she now had to organize daily living to a degree largely unnecessary as a single or partner in a childless marriage. If marriage called for more stability in the migrant's life, the birth of children added new responsibilities and needs that were even more pressing: larger home, higher salary, occupational security, and a clearer, more stable future. In addition, the parent now had to consider where it would be best to rear children, and this required a careful consideration of quality of life concerns. Brian described how his family responsibilities and occupational commitments combined to entrench him in his Australian life. Life, in short, became routinized and satisfactory.

Brian returned to Australia to reunite with his Australian wife. His plan was to return to the States immediately, but he was persuaded to enroll in Melbourne University for a law degree, using the GI Bill benefits. Five years later he decided to stay.

"At any time during the five years did you ever think seriously about returning to the States?" asked the interviewer.

> I think I always intended to return to the States. But during the course of those five years my wife and I had three children, and that made a big difference. And if I'd gone back to the States at that stage, I would have had to do another year of study in order to qualify in any state in the United States as a lawyer. I thought it would be very difficult, so I decided to stay in Australia. I think it's merely that you become involved. You make friends, you start to build a new life, you start having children. And I thought we'd return and as a result I registered the first two children at the American consulate as American citizens. The third daughter I didn't bother with, she was born shortly after I graduated.

The responsibilities of parenthood tended to restrict peoples' perceptions of alternatives to the immediate here-and-now reality of Australia, and reinforced the secure sense that daily life was now routine. Migrants realized that their children were Australians, rather than Americans-living-in-Australia; they would be strangers in America. As children internalized Australian culture, so did the migrant—Australian-rules football (or the "footy"), holidays at the beach, bush walking, and barbecues with grilled lamb chops. Americans became Australians through their children.

This did not imply denial or rejection of ultimate plans to return to the United States, although such plans may have receded into the background of regularly considered options for the future. But lulled into the comfortable habits of daily life, Yanks as parents had less and less cause to consider returning. Many thought that when their children grew older, they would decide for themselves whether to "return" to America. But few ever did. "What would I go back to?" they asked rhetorically. The younger they were when they arrived, the less they had to forget about the "old country." With all their friends living there, with plans for future work and families there, and significantly, with their parents there, even children born in the States often saw no reason to consider leaving Australia.

The question of citizenship became important with the birth of children, especially for those without definite plans for settlement. While Americans could easily ignore the issue of naturalization for themselves (as we shall see later), the problem arose of preserving the choice of citizenship for children, to allow them to decide when they were older. Unless care was taken to secure dual citizenship, Australian-born children would become Australian citizens by default, if one parent was Australian. Citizenship was understood by every Yank to mean a final indication of the intent to settle permanently, and parents, therefore, took care to register their children at the nearest American consulate. This enabled the parents to further postpone the decision to settle in Australia or return to America. Yanks were themselves assured that their children's futures had been broadened by the availability of such a choice. The children commonly retained it as long as possible, up to their 21st birthday, allowing them to visit and work in America for awhile before returning to Australia for "normal life."

In general, most returned Olim (52%) perceived themselves as pushed from Israel in contrast to being pulled back to America (24%), most particularly by difficulties surrounding their familial and instrumental needs. Certainly, these factors support the adjustment model sketched in the previous chapter. Namely, daily life concerns swirling around one's family and institutional needs dominated immigrant adjustment. The religious and ethnic factors lost their saliency. It was this saliency in an American context which led to the original migration decision.

One of the returnees in our sample was Joe, an engineer, who was married with two children. He had lived in Israel for one year but returned due to family factors. Even though he found disadvantages to living in Israel due to "inefficiencies in industry and business, rudeness (of the people), and the climate," none of these would have caused him to return if not for his family situation. As Joe said, "My mother got cancer—she was supposed to visit for Pesach (Passover)—and my sister got divorced. We returned to the States for Pesach and felt we could not leave the family again at that time." Despite his sentiments and situation, Joe indicated at the time of the interview that there was a 75% chance he would return to live in Israel.

OCCUPATIONAL AND INSTRUMENTAL FACTORS (QUADRANT B)

> The appointment was only for three years with guaranteed return. . . . At the end of three years I could return to America with travel expenses being paid. So you could look at it as a three-year post-doctoral stint. As it turned out, I liked working here and I got involved in what I was doing. So I didn't go back at the end of three years.

Yanks who developed commitments to Australian spouses and families, or to friends, often revised their time schedules for returning to the States, if not actually deciding to settle. But unmarried Americans, or those with American spouses, and childless migrants were free from such enticements and pressures. Yet they, too, often remained as settlers, or continuously put off their return. They usually did so because they were satisfied with their employment.

Sojourners gradually changed their orientations toward their work in Australia to a degree that it became impractical to return to the States according to original plans. Either they decided to settle or they made returning contingent on finding work that was similar to their Australian occupational status, a qualification difficult to fulfill. For as they became more deeply involved with work, they realized that their new standards for suitable employment would probably not be met in America. They would have to remain in Australia as long as they were committed to their careers. The reluctance to risk what had been gained in order to return to the United States, with little hope of recovering their career position there, made the prospect of going back unfavorable. Thus, commitments made through work led to de facto settlement even before they actually made decisions to do so.

But unforeseen circumstances could change the importance of work for the sojourner. The responsibilities of marriage to an Australian or the birth of children often exerted pressures to find secure employment, higher pay, and future security. Recruited migrants became entrenched in their jobs to the point of looking on them as permanent. Teachers fresh out of college found this, their first real job, more rewarding than expected. As they became accepted as "permanent staff," they began to see themselves in the same way. Julie, the divorced mother of two from California, had never had a full-time teaching job before arriving at Aspendale Technical School in a Melbourne suburb.

"You came to Australia without deciding to migrate, but before that had you ever thought about migrating?" asked the interviewer. "No, never," replied Julie. "Well, then, when did you start having thoughts about remaining?"

> After I'd been here, oh, six or seven months. I found at Aspendale Tech a place that needed me, at a time in my life when I really needed to be needed. You know, I've described the conditions there. And they needed somebody with an organized mind, somebody who doesn't mind working, who gets in there and does things. That's sort of the way I am, and they needed me, and I fitted in. I felt good here.

Perhaps more important for recruited migrants was that those conditions in Australia that led to overseas recruitment in the first place also provided lucrative opportunities for work and careers in Australia. Migrants who went under contract often found that the conditions of scarcity in their fields provided them with opportunities that could perhaps be exploited outside the sponsoring company. They often struck out on their own, forming their own businesses in Australia once they had completed their contracts, rather than returning to America.

Yanks whose principal objectives were the thrill of travel and the experience of living abroad usually could not afford to be too selective about their jobs and had to keep expectations low enough to take whatever opportunities came their way. But a combination of good fortune, careful job selection, valuable educational backgrounds, and hard work could result in rewarding potential careers. John and Heather went to Australia so he could complete his doctoral degree in mathematics. He was soon offered an attractive university position. They were accustomed to the frugal life of graduate students, and their young son occupied most of Heather's time. She explained how they found professional opportunities beyond their early expectations.

> We anticipated it would take four years to get the Ph.D. And then we came out and liked it. I got a job and liked it very much. We said, "Well, gee, what's the situation overseas?" And we wrote away to a lot of other friends and said, "What would you do in our shoes?" And the answers from two of them were very firm: "Stay in Australia, look at what happens when the general pattern of economic . . . (conditions) goes into a fall and think of what it will be like to be one of many Ph.D.'s in the States who can't get jobs." And so our friends said, "Stay, you'll have a Ph.D. in a country without many Ph.D.'s. Form an economic base, give your son a nice childhood. And then when you finish the Ph.D. move off." So that was one of the reasons that we stayed. And instead of finishing the Ph.D. in 4 years and really pushing it, we said, "Why bother to push and finish it?" John was offered a better job and we were living fairly well. And this job looked very nice, and all of a sudden we'd be in the upper bracket and he could still finish his Ph.D. and it might take five years instead of four. And so I said, "Right!"

Heather soon found a lectureship in a Melbourne-area university and began to pursue her Ph.D. and lecture professionally in another related field—although she had considered doing neither before arriving in Australia.

Americans rarely expected to get rich. Those who ended up in well-paying jobs realized that equivalent work in America paid much more. Few Americans grew wealthy in Australia: The taxes were too high, the loopholes too tight, the wage scale too low, and their competitive drive unappreciated by Australians. However, career opportunities held other attractive rewards. Work was sometimes intrinsically satisfying and rewarding; interesting and challenging with important responsibilities; providing associations with stimulating people, a sense of professionalism, a source of excitement; and offering feelings of personal fulfillment, autonomy, action, and security.

Professionally employed Americans often remarked how they felt they were known for their work country-wide. Recognition by colleagues was due largely to Australia's small population and its concentration in the six or seven major urban areas of the country (half of whom lived in Melbourne and Sydney alone). Such recognition could be a powerful attraction for people who only recently had been anonymous, insecure, and indistinguishable from others back in the States. While aware of the "big frog in the little pond" nature of their reputations, they nevertheless found it extremely satisfying and correspondingly hard to surrender by returning to America. Not only would colleagues in America not have even heard of them, but achievement of a similar level of recognition there was highly unlikely.

Another important source of satisfaction with work was the unexpectedly rapid promotions they sometimes achieved. This was especially significant for recruited migrants who found themselves in a "seller's market" within their occupations. They discovered they could rise in Australia much faster than they could expect to in the States. Academics, for instance, found themselves in tenured university positions much more quickly than was normal in the American academic scene. Many decided to remain indefinitely in order to exploit such opportunities, perhaps to strengthen their bargaining positions for their still-expected return to the States as well. Continued career progress, of course, led to further deferral of plans to return. This nearly happened to one of the authors. Almost by accident, he found a teaching position at Melbourne University that paid well and provided numerous "perks." He was sorely tempted to extend his commitment another year but had already deposited money for a cruise ship to Japan as part of the planned return itinerary six months earlier. He decided against staying. There were many who decided otherwise.

A significant factor in their accelerated occupational progress was their American work ethic. They were accustomed to hard work, ego-involvement in their careers, high standards of quality and efficiency, intense competition, working under pressure, and promotions based on competence. As we noted, they usually found that Australians were much less "driven." Here is Doris again, discussing her "cultural advantage":

> Well, being able to cope . . . you live in New York or Boston or San Francisco, and you have to be able to cope with pressure, and not many Australians can cope with pressure, because they have not really had any previous pressure to deal with (or) to learn from.

The American work ethic had its disadvantages as well, colliding with the more relaxed "she'll be right" Australian attitude that often led to significant adjustment problems. But it typically led to faster promotions and more career opportunities. Yanks were often better trained than Australians, giving them an edge in at least the initial stages of their careers. For instance, advertising executives found themselves better prepared and schooled in the most advanced techniques than Australians. So ingrained was the American work ethic that some who ended up settling in Australia also found themselves, like Doris, working for American corporations, and finding the atmosphere more comfortable and familiar.

Ironically, then, the American work ethic was both an important source of adjustment problems, as well as an important factor in deciding to settle. Yanks became tied to Australia because of their involvement in their work.

Yanks with strong occupational ties would find it much more difficult to leave, by a 9 to 1 margin. Those with average to weak ties would find it hard to leave, by about a 2 to 1 margin. Regardless of the particular nature of their occupational satisfaction, they faced new and unexpected questions of whether to pursue their careers in Australia or return to the United States where their opportunities seemed less inviting. Although now unmarried and childless, Budd knew that it would be prohibitively difficult to get started in America as an independent commercial artist.

> I'd love to go back. It's not feasible, but I'd like to go back in a minute. I'd love to because I like the air, the type of thinking that's going on. But there's no way. I'm totally independent. I want to continue working. How can you continue working? The cost of getting refinanced and setting up a business or working on your own?

When the commitments of work, family, marriage, and friendships merged together, they formed a powerful bond to the country. Yanks without families or Australian spouses found that work had become so central to their sense of well-being that return to America had no apparent advantages.

The instrumental process of readjusting to the United States for returned Olim was, understandably, smoother than adjusting to daily life in Israel. But things were not quite the same after living in Israel: 71% of the returnee group reported that life seemed significantly different in America in comparison to what it seemed before their migration. Even though 53% of the returnees perceived themselves as more involved in the American Jewish community than before, "their hearts were still in the East." Indeed, four fifths of returnees (79%) stated there was a 50–50 chance or better that they might return to Israel and, likewise, 80% reported presently having Israeli friends in America.

Waxman and Appel (1986), utilizing the categorization originally developed by Dashefsky and Lazerwitz (1983), reported similar findings for a "snowball sample" of 71 returned emigrants studied in 1983. However, Waxman and Appel, in probing the respondents' motivations for return with open-ended questions rather than handing them a preset list, found that the bureaucracy of Israeli society was cited much less frequently, unlike the findings of Antonovsky and Katz (1979), Avruch (1981), and Jubas (1974).

Further analysis of the perceptions of the returnees revealed that while most saw themselves as pulled to Israel (77%) rather than pushed from the United States (44%), most also saw themselves as pushed from Israel (52%) rather than pulled to return to the United States (24%). In other words, it was more than twice as likely for Olim to perceive themselves as pushed rather than pulled in leaving Israel.

Harry had lived in Israel for two years and was interviewed four years after his return. His major reason for returning was financial considerations. "It is very expensive to live in Israel. It would be easier with an American income from a government pension. I returned to put the few more years in for the pension." Nevertheless, he concluded that there was a 75% chance, in his estimate, that he would go back to live there again.

POLITICAL COMMITMENT (QUADRANT A)

"Are you an American citizen?" asked the interviewer. "Oh, certainly! I wouldn't give that up. No, uh uh! I was in the damn Navy. I deserve it. I'll keep it, you know. Put in some time for them, did the right thing by them."

"Have you ever thought about taking out Australian citizenship?" continued the interviewer. "Never thought about it. No reason whatsoever," concluded Alan, an American emigrant of ten years.

The perception of American emigration has often had a distinct political tinge. One popular belief was that Americans migrated out of political disenchantment with America. Many assumed that Americans who lived abroad for an extended period of time had rejected America in some political sense. They had turned their backs on their country, were no longer loyal Americans, or perhaps were even disloyal ones. And the issue of changing from American to some other citizenship seemed to imply a transfer of political allegiances as well, not to mention the deep emotions such citizenship exchanges usually stirred for participants and American observers alike. Finally, the assumptions about American migration inherent in both media and professional literature typically pointed to political as well as economic decisions being involved in the move, since the term "American" is often used both as a political and a sociocultural identity tag.

Yanks and Citizenship

Early interviews revealed that most Yanks were not politically motivated in their decisions to move; that they were not even politically conscious, or at least not particularly so; and that they saw no political relevance to their decisions to settle. Even Americans who became naturalized Australians tended to see the issue in pragmatic rather than political terms. In fact, an apparent paradox emerged, since many who had lived in Australia for as long as 20 years often maintained that they were now even more patriotically American than ever before. Conversely, even among those who had become Australian citizens, there appeared to be little political allegiance to Australia. Finifter and Finifter (1989) found in their study of 290 Americans in Australia that the longer the Yanks lived in their adopted country, the more likely they were to have a political party preference there. For the vast majority of Americans, America remained the focus of political awareness, identity, and allegiance—if they ever considered the matter at all.

Political allegiance was related to length of residence, with about one in three of the earliest arrivals (1959 or earlier) claiming strong Australian loyalties compared with one in five of the 1970-and-later arrivals. Interestingly, about one out of three who had lived in Australia for 15 years or longer still felt strong political allegiance to the States. Overall, however, most held only average to weak ties to either country, suggesting that questions of political loyalties were irrelevant to decisions to remain or return.

Migrants found that their American identities were common topics of conversation, but not so much in a political connotation. They were reminded of their nationality by references to their speech, but rarely encountered allusions to it as an issue of political loyalties. Political ideology was just not important. Settlement resulted from social and occupational involvements, because the responsibilities and satisfactions of marriage, parenthood, and work comprised the basic activities of daily living.

About three out of four respondents felt strong social ties to the country. But such ties did not necessarily indicate corresponding political ties, for those who claimed strong political ties were balanced by the same proportion claiming weak ones. Conversely, nobody with strong Australian political ties admitted to weak social ties. Social ties were far more easily made and far more meaningful than political allegiances.

Political ideologies and loyalties were simply too far removed from the concerns of daily life to have any real importance in decision making. It was only when we deliberately broached the topic of political allegiance that respondents commented on political matters, and then almost always in such a way as to strongly suggest that they had given little consideration to the issue. Once "forced" to consider the question of political identity, migrants organized their responses around one or more themes. One common response was a defensive reaction, an insistence that their decisions to migrate or settle were not politically motivated and did not imply any rejection of America. They were still loyal Americans. But "loyalty to America" was difficult to explain or define. Some manufactured hypothetical situations, for example, "If America and Australia went to war with each other . . . " They would explain why they would favor the American side. Chris had lived in Australia for nearly 30 years, and had been away from the United States even longer than that. Nonetheless, she still admitted a basic allegiance to the States, and explained why.

> I don't think everything U.S.-wise is a hundred percent. I think there are many things where it's found wanting. But it is an interesting nation and a nation to which I shall always be loyal because I feel so much of what I am came from the U.S. originally. It gave my migrant parents the opportunity to give us tremendous opportunities. These opportunities I have had and have been able to draw on over a lifetime. And I am very grateful to the U.S. for it, and I'll always be loyal to the U.S., whatever happens to it. I won't let anyone run it down too far.

Everybody had a different way of trying to define political identity, basically because political allegiance had no practical or tangible meaning. Political loyalties were emotional and abstract, not clearly manifest in daily activities.

A second thematic response included some kind of discussion of America's political scene, often with an apology for America's role in world politics. Since the Vietnam War was over by the time of the interviews, the most important international event involving the United States was negotiations in the Middle East, and the media's attention to this had the overall effect of instilling migrants with a sense of admiration for their country. Whether or not they were critical of American political activities, migrants usually affirmed their faith in their native country. Julie, the teacher at Aspendale Tech, was deeply involved in local left-wing politics in California before going to Australia. She was a strong critic of Nixon-Reagan, conservative politics, and a firm opponent of the Vietnam War. Still, she felt pride in her country.

> I miss not being part of the American political scene. I was very politically aware and involved. Now I'm very unaware of the small world of politics, the county, the states, you know. It's very hard to get these kinds of things. So I do lose contact, and I do try to keep up, and I am concerned a bit. I'm more concerned with America and its image than I ever have been, how people feel about it. I'm very defensive at times. You know, I don't believe "my country right or wrong, my country," but I mean, it is my country. I am part of it.

Indeed, we found few who totally disavowed their American heritage or who felt politically alienated from the United States.

A third popular theme was the expression of total indifference to politics of either the American or Australian variety. Such people felt no political interest in or affiliation with either country. However, there was very little political alienation. For settlement involved and implied no political realignments, and was not inconsistent with strong feelings of loyalty to the United States. This helps to explain the reluctance of Americans to becoming naturalized Australian citizens.

Americans have the lowest naturalization rate of any major migration group in Australia. Richmond (1967) also notes that Americans have the lowest rates of Canadian naturalization, and explains it in terms of "status dislocation," or cultural dissimilarities between the "old country" and Canada. The more similar the countries, he says, the less of a break in the migrant's way of life, and the less likely he or she is to be forced to sever ties with the old country. He argues that there is an inverse relationship between the degree of effort of adjustment and strength of identity with the new country. That is, people who are not forced to make a clear cultural choice by living in Canada and do not become strongly tied to that country are not persuaded to change their citizenship.

Our data tend to support Richmond's argument. Americans typically suffered few adjustment problems and generally perceived a strong similarity between Australia and America. We do not have direct evidence of migrants' psychological orientation, so we must stop short of full agreement with his conclusions. Actually, Richmond did not have such data either. He imputed his psychological explanation from nonpsychological survey data (which only showed a statistical relationship between rates of naturalization and nationality).

The matter of citizenship was at once of central importance and general indifference to Americans in Australia. More accurately, citizenship was such an emotionally potent issue that few gave naturalization serious thought, even people who were obviously going to settle. Citizenship meant much the same things to most. First, and most important, it was the emotional link to what may be called the American Heritage. To sever this link meant to be cut off from America in a way that distance and prolonged absence could not match. Migrants found it difficult to explain precisely the emotional bond signified by citizenship. So the typical response to the question, "Have you ever thought of becoming an Australian citizen?" was an emphatic "No!"

It was clear as we listened to them that they had answered reflexively and spontaneously and that their rationales were simply afterthoughts. For instance, they frequently mentioned the fear that by losing their citizenship they would have trouble getting back to America should they want to return for social visits, to attend a sick or dead parent, or to return to the States. Their obviously strong feelings were rooted in more than rational arguments. They simply could not seriously entertain the idea of exchanging citizenship.

Of course, it is also understandable that the sojourners did not consider Australian citizenship, just as they did not initially consider permanent residence.

Settlers, people who had originally intended to stay permanently, accounted for most who had already applied for or definitely would apply for citizenship. However, two out of five settlers stated they would probably or definitely not become Australian citizens.

We tried hard to locate and interview Americans who had taken the final step of naturalization. They varied widely in age, length of residence, occupation, marital status, initial settlement intentions, and reasons for changing citizenship. Brian's 1946 visit to Australia was expected to be brief, but he became committed to his career and his family, and continued to defer the decision to return. After spending five arduous years of training to become a solicitor (or lawyer) at Melbourne University, he was forced to make the crucial decision.

> Shortly after commencing my Articles (a kind of apprenticeship) I learned that because I was an American I would have to change my citizenship to Australian because we had to swear allegiance to the Crown. I changed it about a week before I was admitted to the bar.

"How did you feel about changing your citizenship?" asked the interviewer.

> I think it was a very big step for me to take. I loathed doing it. I preferred being an American living in Australia. I mean, being an American you have a great regard for your home. I suppose that applies to all people who change their citizenship during their lifetime. I certainly did not like it. It was a matter of wanting to use the knowledge I had gained after five years of study and several more years of work in the commercial world. I wanted to do what I felt was best to do. I thought Australia was my home forever more. Although I loathed doing it, I felt it was the only right thing to do.

Dave and his wife Sue were cotton farmers. They became Australian citizens as soon as they were eligible. Like Brian (the solicitor), they had very pragmatic reasons for doing so.

> We're all Australian citizens. You can't afford to own land in Australia and live here and be a U.S. citizen, because they both tax you if you die on death duties, at the full rate on the original evaluation. Not after one of them takes it out. So end up you're bound to lose at least 75% of your holdings between them. That is one thing. The other thing is I'm engaged in, you might say, business politics. In other words, I'm chairman of the co-op, represent the co-op on matters at the political level, business levels. And at first when starting something new and your technology is coming from the U.S., it's probably an asset rather than a liability. But after a time this shifts because they then decide that they're experts on it, not somebody else. And also you become suspect as to why you didn't join the mob. So everything put together, just seemed better, went right ahead and became Australians. And also you can vote and say what you think and then do something about it. There was never any pressure on us to become citizens.

These diverse explanations make it possible to say only that Americans changed their citizenship to Australian for very personal and usually very practical reasons. It was clear that naturalization was the culmination of the settlement process. Americans who became Australian citizens had taken the exceptional step of making public and visible their status as settlers. They had reached a decision that most other migrants were reluctant consciously to make. They had decided firmly and, in their eyes, irrevocably to settle. Unlike the others, they retained no options. They had decided to do what many ended up doing anyway without really deciding.

Olim and Citizenship

There are two factors that affect American immigrants to Israel regarding their citizenship status. The first is the motivation for migration. The second is the corpus of Israeli laws and American judicial decisions that have an impact on dual citizenship.

Inasmuch as most Americans coming to Israel are migrating for ideological reasons, they are generally interested in fully participating in the Israeli political process. This includes serving in the army and accepting Israeli citizenship. Until 1968, however, American authorities interpreted acceptance of Israeli citizenship as an indication of loyalty to a foreign power, and therefore revoked American citizenship from those who became Israeli nationals. Isaacs (1966) reported on how difficult a decision it then was for Olim. However, a U.S. Supreme Court decision in 1968 (Efroyim vs. Rusk) led to a recognition of dual nationality for those persons who passively receive foreign citizenship. In the Israeli case this means that persons who receive Israeli citizenship without having asked for it do not automatically lose their American citizenship.

Following the Supreme Court decision, most Americans now passively accept Israeli citizenship once their allowed term as a temporary resident expires. The procedure is a technical one. The Ministry of Interior issues an immigrant visa after the end of the three-year period during which temporary resident visas are freely issued. At that time the immigrant is informed that he or she will automatically become a citizen unless a waiver form is filled out within a three-month period. The applicant signs a form acknowledging this fact. After that period elapses, the citizen merely receives a new identity booklet that lists his or her citizenship as Israeli. There is no swearing in ceremony of any type marking this transition, as there is in the United States. The Ministry even issues a certificate upon request stating the provision under which citizenship was granted, and this is recognized by the United States as indicating passive acceptance of citizenship. From that point on, Israeli Americans are subject to the laws of two states. These can include the requirement to register with the military of both countries, as well as to file annual income tax returns in Israel and in the United States. It is not uncommon to see such persons traveling with two passports, one American and one Israeli. American Israelis are also entitled to vote in the elections of both countries. There have even been cases of American Israelis elected to the Knesset or Israeli Parliament. As a rule, Americans routinely register their children born in Israel with the United States consulate and exchange their Israeli birth certificate for a "Report of a Birth Abroad of a United States Citizen."

Not all Americans accept Israeli citizenship, even after the change in the law. The feeling of some of these persons is that laws and regulations can change or be reinterpreted and why risk their American citizenship or American social security. Some ultra-Orthodox, or *haredi*, Jews also opt out of Israeli citizenship for ideological reasons. Their move to Israel is based on strictly religious grounds, and they do not support the political entity of the secular state of Israel.

It is interesting that persons who consciously desire to live in another country should be so concerned about their citizenship as are Americans in Israel and Australia. It is much more convenient to travel with an American passport, not only to the United States, but throughout the world as well, than with an Israeli or Australian passport. For example, there is so much concern with American citizenship among Olim that special migration emissaries from Israel (or *shlihim*) in the United States have reported being questioned by young couples as to how American citizenship laws would affect their grandchildren, although they did not yet even have any children!

It must be emphasized that the Americans in Israel are content to retain an American passport because they do so very much retain an American identity. Whereas they were Jews in the United States, they are Americans in Israel. Having said this, though, we must point out that this identity is a relative one and is highlighted when they are in Israel. To some extent their American identification manifests itself more culturally than politically.

There are many manifestations of an American cultural identity in Israel. It appears in dress, manners, food preferences, and interest in American current events. The English-language *Jerusalem Post* carries American sports prominently for its readers. Thanksgiving and the American Independence Day are celebrated by members of the Association of Americans and Canadians in Israel. American board games, such as Trivial Pursuit, have a wide following among American expatriates. Overall we would argue that while one can take Americans out of America, it is more difficult to take America out of the Americans.

Finally, the question arises as to whether any self-expressive aspects of the experience of living in Israel and the distinctive characteristics of the leavers as compared to the stayers influenced their subsequent life in the United States. Our study of the returnees revealed that seven out of ten (71%) indicated that their life in the United States was different after their return from what it was before they left. Nevertheless, there was virtually no change in the returnees' sense of being more Jewish than American with 74% feeling this way before emigration and 72% after their return. A majority (53%) saw themselves as more involved in the

American Jewish community. Interestingly, only 38% reported attending religious services twice monthly or more, compared to 54% who did so before migration. If religious services were not as important a dimension in their Jewish lives, having Israeli friends was. Eighty percent of the returnees reported having Israeli friends, compared to 60% so reporting before migration. Israeli friends and, indeed, Israel seemed to constitute a larger part of their lives after their return.

Because the leavers were less traditional in their pattern of Jewish identification than the stayers (as pointed out in a previous section), it is not surprising that the returnees reported a decrease in synagogue attendance. Therefore, the way in which their perceived greater involvement in the American Jewish community manifested itself was likely through Jewish social and cultural experiences, such as speaking Hebrew, or talking about Israel to Israeli friends, or sending their children to a Jewish day school.[4] Because these characteristics were highly atypical for the American Jewish community, they highlighted the returnees' Jewish involvement.

Indeed, Sam had lived in Israel for three years. He was interviewed two years after his return at age 49, married with two children. He found many difficulties in everyday life and found a lack of ethical values. Sam "expected to find middle-class Jewish American values. . . . This is not so. . . . Everybody is scratching for a living . . . and at everyone's throat. . . . The little amenities of life are missing . . . and I'm too old to live that way," he concluded. Indeed, he attached a very low probability to the notion of ever returning to live in Israel.

All of these manifestations notwithstanding, as stated earlier, four fifths of returnees said there was a 50–50 chance or better that they would return to live in Israel. Despite the fact that many expressed feelings of anger or embarrassment about their Israel experience, a great majority of returnees were still thinking about living in Israel! This suggests the potential repetitiveness of emigration or reemigration as part of the full understanding of the migration cycle (see Bovenkerk, 1974; Scott and Scott, 1989, p. 24).

In sum, for most migrants, their return is facilitated by the absence of a fundamental break with the United States when they initially left. When some of them fail to find enough "extra plus" to offset the difficulties they encounter, there is an inclination to return to the United States. The lack of a routinized and satisfactory life in Israel offers very little to keep them there and aids in a return to the United States. Once back, they must seek to readjust to the American Jewish community from which they originally felt somewhat estranged. Since they are not affluent (which might have made it easier to remain in Israel), most cannot command the influence to be the top leaders in the mainstream organiza-

---

[4]Waxman (1989, p. 182) reported a similar finding in his sample of 71 returned Olim. He noted among them a strong interest in Jewish day school enrollment for their children.

tions of community life, such as the synagogue and federation. Nevertheless, they contribute significantly to various compatible aspects of organized American Jewish life, such as day schools. Informally they associate with others who have had similar experiences as well as Israelis living in the United States. The returnees, however, once more manage to keep some distance from the organizations and leadership of the American Jewish community. Also, for a large majority of such returned migrants the desirability of going back to Israel is still fairly high. As one returnee who returned to join the family business stated, "My heart is in Israel, but my status (job) is here in the U.S."

SUMMARY

In this chapter the study of the migration cycle is completed by examining the factors that influenced the decision to remain in the host society or return to the United States. The findings are drawn from the surveys conducted in Australia and Israel as well as a special sample of migrants who returned to the United States from Israel, called returnees. An assessment of the rates of staying (and returning) put the phenomenon in the proper context. Analysis of changes in the number of Americans in Israel between the 1961 and 1972 Israeli censuses indicated that the percentage staying was 42% and that in the 1961–1982 period it had risen to around 48%. The corresponding two periods in Australia showed a decline. For the 1961–1970 period, the staying rate was 48% and for the longer 1961–1981 period the rate of those remaining declined to 25%.

Whereas motivation for migration tended to cluster in quadrant A, self-expressive ones, and adjustments in quadrant B, self-instrumental concerns, the cross-pressures to remain or return focused predominantly on quadrant C, others-expressive issues, such as marriage, familial reunification, family harmony, and education of the children. At a secondary level were the self-instrumental areas of quadrant B, such as occupational concerns, local bureaucracy, housing, and daily living needs. In fact, the self-expressive factors of quadrant A, which were so influential in motivating migration, were of tertiary importance and focused on political or citizenship concerns. Very little evidence was found of quadrant D, others-instrumental factors, playing an important role in the issue of remaining or returning. A small proportion of returned Americans from Israel cited military service as a factor in their return.

Just as there has been some confusion (not to say total misunderstanding) about how and why Yanks decided to go to Australia, there is little appreciation for why they stayed there. The assumption has been widespread that they remained because they intended all along to stay. But most did not intend to migrate, in the sense of what this term implies to most people. Most who have settled did not originally intend to do so. Somehow they became settlers. Indeed, most who returned to the States—as most did—intended all along to go back home. It is easy to assume "rejection of America" and "rejection of Australia" as explanations of why Americans move to or return from Australia.

Settling was usually not a political or ideological decision. It meant new families, homes, and jobs, but not new political loyalties. Yanks rarely confronted the sensitive issues of citizenship. Their decisions to stay emerged from their recognition and acceptance of circumstances that now bound them to a new future. Furthermore, their decisions to stay were often made by default, rather than by design. That is, the typical question facing these Yanks was "why go back?" rather than "why stay?"

Thus, the process of settling was not a completed one, leading to an unambiguous identity of settler. Migrants who had lived there for 20 years or longer were still reluctant to commit themselves firmly to remaining for the rest of their lives. They qualified their intentions, made them tentative and conditional upon hypothetical events or contingencies. They rarely formalized their intentions by taking out Australian citizenship, and then only for very pragmatic purposes. For most, the process was an ongoing one, a kind of subtle and tender trap.

In the case of Olim, most saw themselves as pushed from Israel rather than pulled back to America, with family factors representing the greatest pressure, followed by concerns about jobs, bureaucracy, housing, and the like. Political and communal concerns represented a lesser level of concern followed by issues related to military service. The returned Olim, the returnees, expressed both extropunitive responses, such as anger at Israel for failing them, or intropunitive responses, such as embarrassment in their having failed at their chosen heroic task. Nevertheless, the great majority of returnees said there was a better than 50–50 chance they would return to live in Israel. Perhaps the migration cycle is never complete as some were ready at some future time to resume their odyssey.

8

Summary and Conclusions

Emigrants from American society tend to be shadowy and elusive whereas immigrants are highly visible and identifiable individuals within the culture. This is not surprising in a society built on the cultural myth of being a haven for the "wretched refuse" of another country's teeming shore. Such a tribute, enshrined in the symbol of the United States, the Statue of Liberty, doubtlessly inspired millions of immigrants who passed by her, as well as millions who aspired to throw off the yoke of oppression.

What is interesting is the fact that American sociologists seeking to understand and explain the nature of human behavior and unfettered by conventional biases have greatly neglected to focus their attention on emigration in comparison to the study of immigration. Perhaps this is so because so many sociological researchers interested in this topic have themselves tended to come from immigrant backgrounds that led them to focus more on immigration than emigration. Furthermore, the American experience has been colored by the kind of optimism that inspired the poetry inscribed on the Statue of Liberty. America is the best of all possible worlds and emigration is not consistent with that optimism. Finally, the functionalist model that traditionally dominated this type of inquiry assumed the assimilation of immigrants to be inevitable.

According to the *Cumulative Index of Sociology Journals* (Lantz, 1987), the major journals covered in this volume published 49 articles and reviews on immigrants and immigration during 1971–1985. In the corresponding period, only seven articles were published on the topic of emigrants and emigration. In other words, the scholarly interest in immigrants was seven times greater than the corresponding interest in emigrants. This finding is all the more curious considering that the volume of immigrants (approximately 30 million) entering the United States was only three times the volume of emigrants (approximately 10 million) leaving the United States in the first three quarters of the twentieth century as was noted at the outset of this book. This study sheds new light on a puzzling question of emigration: Why do Americans leave America and resettle elsewhere, for example, Australia and Israel?

REVIEW OF FINDINGS

Chapter 1 presents the issue of migration as one of the central themes affecting the transformation of human societies, and indeed the existence of humanity, since earliest times. International migration was noted as being different from internal migration because of the generally greater distances, cultural, legal, and linguistic obstacles faced by the migrants. Classical explanations of such migration have focused on the "push-pull" dynamics. This approach is rooted in a functional model that views human behavior as part of a systemic whole. The approach in this study, however, focuses on individuals as the units of analysis rather than the society, the system, the group, or even the life space. The result is an explanation based on the cognitive, affective, and evaluative processes that permit human beings the opportunity to interpret their experience.

As was also noted in Chapter 1, the major existing weakness of the migration literature is the difficulty in explaining why *people* move. In this study an attempt was made to answer this and related social psychological questions, at least for voluntaristic international migration centered on ideology, personal fulfillment, or family relationships. With the breakdown of political and economic barriers emerging in the 1990s in Europe, hitherto thought to be impermeable because of long-standing interregional hostility and enmity, this kind of migration may become much more common than the 5–7% it is estimated to represent of total international migration in the generation after World War II. In this context, this study sought to investigate the motivations for migration, adjustments in the host country, and the factors in return migration within a social psychological perspective.

Chapter 2 argued that immigration produces emigration as a normal repercussion. The former represents the flood tide and the latter the associated ebb. Seven countries received 88% of this outward flow of emigrants: Mexico, Germany, United Kingdom, Canada, Japan, Australia, and Israel. Following the approach of Emile Durkheim in his classic work of *Suicide* (1951), it was argued that emigration is the result of detachment. Emigrants were hypothesized as being weakly bound to their existing social relationships. On this basis, a table was constructed arraying the goals of migration ("expressive" and "instrumental") on the horizontal axis and the locus of concern ("self" or "other") on the vertical axis. Therefore, in quadrant A, self-expressive motivations include individuals seeking greater political or religious expression or wanderers. Quadrant B, self-instrumental motives, referred to migrant laborers, students, or the so-called "brain drain" workers. Quadrant C, others-expressive motivations, included disciples of charismatic leaders, adherents of religious and political groups, or simply spouses and children seeking family unity. Finally, quadrant D, others-instrumental motives, referred to such types as Peace Corps volunteers or religious missionaries. This Cartesian coordinate system served as a model for the organization of the empirical data of the current study in subsequent chapters as well, which examined motivations, adjustments, and return migration of Americans who went abroad with the declared intention of staying in the receiving country for more than a year.

Ideally, the optimal method of conducting such a study would be to administer similar questionnaires to probability samples of American emigrants in as many of the seven countries mentioned above as possible. Since the financial and administrative obstacles to such an approach are formidable, a more limited strategy was utilized, namely, analyzing comparable data sets available to the researchers for at least two countries with similar patterns of substantial voluntary international migration of Americans: Australia and Israel. A variety of data sources and methods was utilized approximating the technique of triangulation including survey research relying both on questionnaires and in-depth interviews, secondary analysis, as well as participant observation.

While Americans have never been a particularly large segment of migrants either to Australia (where they ranked fourteenth in 1982) or Israel (where they ranked seventh in 1972), their numbers began to grow in the late 1960s and peaked in the early 1970s with 6,564 emigrants to Australia in 1972 and 7,364 emigrants to Israel in 1971. By 1982 there were 32,620 Americans in Australia and 37,327 in Israel in 1983. During the 1980s, however, the number of American emigrants moving to Australia sharply declined to between 1,200 and 1,900 annually, and in Israel it fell to between 2,300 and 3,500 annually. A more substantial stream continued to flow to Canada, but the Canadian case was not pursued because it lacked the distinctive elements of international migration posed above.

While the peak of such American emigration corresponds to the political, economic, and cultural dislocations created by the Vietnam War in the late 1960s and early 1970s, the subsequent analysis of the migrants' experiences does not suggest that these anomic pushes played a substantial role. The subsequent chapters revealed the important factors in motivation, adjustment, and return migration. While the Australian data permitted a more qualitative approach, the Israeli data permitted a more quantitative analysis.

Chapters 3 and 4 explored the motives for migration of American emigrants to Australia, the "Yanks," and to Israel, the "Olim." Following Kohn (1987), this study sought to uncover the similarities and differences in the cross-national comparison of American emigrants in Australia and Israel. In general, both the Yanks and Olim resembled each other on a variety of characteristics examined including age, marital status, level of formal education, and employment. They resembled each other much more than the American population as a whole in that they were much younger, slightly less likely to be married, more highly educated and more likely to be professionally employed than Americans in general. Only in one area was there an apparent difference. Males predominated among the Yanks whereas females were more numerous among the Olim.

Most Yanks expressed the desire for adventure, travel, and the challenge of life in another country. Only a minority of Americans expressed a sense of alienation from American society and culture as factors in their move. At the time of their arrival, about two thirds of Yanks expected that they would return to the United States. Similarly, the Olim did not express alienation from American society as much as estrangement from the American Jewish community which led them to seek greater religioethnic fulfillment and expression of their Jewish identity. The majority expressed the view that living in Israel permitted them to live a more complete Jewish life. While the primary motivation for migration for Yanks was the search for adventure and travel and for Olim religioethnic identity fulfillment, these modal responses were similar in that they represented self-expressive motives. Both groups were characteristically young and educated adults who had not yet set down roots and were thus free to exploit an opportunity.

Significant but less prominent motivations for both Yanks and Olim were the self-instrumental goals involving job opportunities, entrepreneurship, or schooling and others-expressive goals, centering on family unity and the spouse's desire to return to his or her homeland. The least popular motivations for migration were others-instrumental in which a small number of Olim migrated to serve as medical or educational personnel or missionaries, notably American rabbis of non-Orthodox denominations.

Chapter 5 reported on the adaptation of the Yanks and Olim in their new societies. This stage of adjustments was interim to the two decisions migrants need to make: first, whether to emigrate, and second, whether to remain or return. In general, the adjustments of the Yanks appeared somewhat easier than for the Olim, who had to contend with a new language, rather than the English the Australians spoke, and a new culture that was not an Anglo variation. Perhaps that is why the Olim were only half as likely as other non-American arrivals to say they would definitely stay in Israel.

In explaining motivations for migration in Chapter 3, self-expressive factors, including the search for adventure or travel, the quest for religioethnic identity and self-fulfillment, or the response to alienation, predominated among the respondents. Self-instrumental issues, however, were most salient in dealing with the adjustment challenges (see Figure 8.1), focusing on jobs, housing, and the standard of living. For a few, others-instrumental motifs of military service, medical care for the family, or corporate transfers were important. Once these instrumental concerns were resolved, individuals turned their attention to the

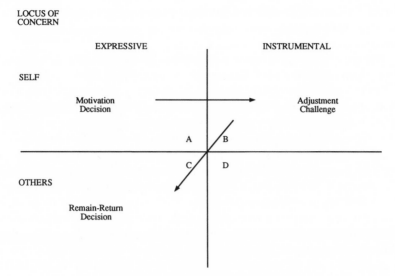

Figure 8.1. The dynamics of emigration.

others-expressive dimensions. As they continued this adjustment phase, the emigrants began to negotiate their remaining major decision whether to remain or return home.

Chapter 6 compared Australian and Israeli differences and similarities with particular attention to settlement outcomes, concluding:

1. Marriage, particularly to a native, promotes staying.
2. Family ties in the new country encourage staying.
3. Satisfaction with one's job and the standard of living facilitates staying.
4. Migration due to the adventure motive increases the likelihood of leaving. (Certain religioethnic experiences increase the likelihood of staying.)
5. The perception of being more at home in the new country encourages staying.
6. Sex ratios vary with men predominant in staying in Australia and women in Israel.

Staying is largely a function of successful integration into the new society—usually intended by Olim, often inadvertent by Yanks. It is important to note that the factors that lead individuals to emigrate from the United States do not substantially affect the experience of the migrants on arrival in the new country and the subsequent decision to stay or leave. This appears to be so even though most

Olim are motivated to emigrate by shared ideological commitments to a religioethnic heritage and most Yanks by personal preferences for adventure and travel and with no initial intention of staying.

The data on the Olim permit an attempt to develop a model of the dynamics of American emigration as follows:

1. This model suggests that absorption is affected by a set of demographic factors, for example, age (over 30), gender (in the case of Israel, being female), and marital status (being married).
2. Staying (or leaving) is next affected by certain background factors prior to migration, such as knowledge of the language (Hebrew in the case of Israel) and organizational involvement (with specific Jewish religioethnic organizations).
3. Experiences in the new society next affect absorption, such as contacts with veteran settlers and satisfactions with various basic areas of daily life including work, housing, and the like.
4. Finally, all of the preceding experiences lead to the most important variable in explaining whether the emigrants stay, and that is "confidence of remaining."

This model, generally including most of the above variables, is likely to apply to a variety of other cases of international migration in the developed world where emigrants move from a country with a higher standard of living to one with a lower one. Of course, the values of some variables may be different as in the case of step 1 for Australia, where being male may be more important than being female is for Israel; but the variable of gender is still likely to be significant. In addition, while the specific language knowledge referred to in step 2 may vary (Hebrew above), the variable of knowledge of the language of the new country will likely persist.

In dealing with their new experiences, both Yanks and Olim have to contend with a lower standard of living and have some difficulties in their adjustment. Many, however, overcome them, and one half of Olim and one quarter of Yanks remain in their new country despite these hardships.

Both Yanks and Olim exhibit a greater concern with work efficiency and quality than their new compatriots. Furthermore, the American emigrants are very achievement oriented, with high expectations for productivity, and this serves them well in advancement in the new society. Despite their newfound success they continue their interest in American life and endeavor to retain their citizenship in the United States. In general, these emigrants appear to be exemplars of American economic, political, and social values. Unlike societies in the developing world where citizens of the United States earned the title of the "ugly Americans," those emigrating abroad in the developed world, at least to Australia and Israel, appear to have earned the title, the "beautiful Americans." This is likely to be the case where there is a shared set of values between the United States and the host country, which the emigrants appear to embody.

Chapter 7 examined the factors involved in the decision to remain in the new society or return to the United States. As presented in Figure 8.1, others-expressive factors predominated in quadrant C, accounting for whether the emigrants chose to remain or return. The pressures that were preeminent included marriage, familial reunification and harmony, as well as a concern for the education of the children. These were followed by self-instrumental concerns such as those dealing with jobs, housing, bureaucracy, and daily living. Finally, issues of a self-expressive nature that dealt with citizenship and politics, community, and cultural aspects of life were least important. Others-instrumental factors were virtually nonexistent.

Over the period covering three censuses in both Australia and Israel between the early 1960s and 1980s, 25% of Yanks remained in Australia and 48% of Olim in Israel. Yanks who had initially intended to settle generally remained. Most Yanks, however, returned to the States because they had always intended to do so and had somehow avoided the unforeseen circumstances of the "tender trap." Olim, on the other hand, generally were more likely to remain in Israel than Yanks in Australia because they had always intended to settle unless unforeseen circumstances prevented them from doing so.

THEORETICAL AND RESEARCH IMPLICATIONS

This research effort has focused on the social psychological factors influencing American migrants in their decisions to move to Australia or Israel and to stay in or return from these countries. In Chapter 2, we hypothesized that most migrating Americans were weakly integrated into American society because they lacked enough of those social characteristics and relationships that bind them to this society. In particular, these inadequate social bonds ought to be those that typically serve to connect people to families of origin, their local communities, or to the United States as a nation.

This exploratory study sought to determine (1) the migrants' motives for moving, (2) the social mechanics guiding their degree of adjustment in their new societies, and (3) the dimensions of their decision to stay in their new societies or to return to the United States and to a limited extent the nature of the reentry process.

It has become clear that emigration, at least in the developed world, is not a static process. Where emigration is involuntary, due to various economic, political, cultural, or religious factors, there is very little likelihood of return. But where emigration is voluntary and migrants are affluent, as in the situation reported in this volume, the possibility for return migration exists. Hence, it is reasonable to characterize this form of international migration as dynamic since there are few "once-and-for-all" decisions. Indeed, for many individuals emigration assumes a cyclical nature entailing emigration, return migration, and at least the possibility of reemigration, as Bovenkerk (1974) termed it.

What differentiates the Australian from the Israeli migrants are the ideological and identity factors. The Yanks were primarily drawn to an English-speaking society. They lacked restraining roots of community, family, and career. They were eager to experiment with life, but religious and subcultural experiences were rarely among their thoughts.

The Olim, however, were primarily motivated by their wish to maximize religious and Jewish cultural experiences. This was no working holiday, but rather a serious search for meaning. As with the Yanks, they usually lacked the social restraints of mature adulthood. Thus, they, too, could indulge in a period of transience.

In short, the emigrants have experienced a loss of personal root connections to combinations of childhood family, local community, or their religioethnic community. This freed them to react to new options. Those going into Australia came upon this option rather unexpectedly in their lives and decided to go for a time of adventure within an English-speaking, Anglo-culture society.

Those going to Israel found themselves free to make this move but not by any unexpected decision. Rather, these Israel-bound migrants have had such an option introduced to them for a number of years. Typically, they have been on one or more visits to Israel and have experienced a taste of life in that society. As a result, many of the Olim were activating a long thought about, and planned for, desire. Some of them, as with those bound for Australia, were suddenly free to move and, hence, decided on the adventure that living in Israel would provide. Yet, even for them, Israel represented an attractive society bringing increased religioethnic satisfactions.

Therefore, the hypothesis given in Chapter 2 is almost, but not quite, fully supported. Although the emigrants were not enmeshed in community, family, and career in the United States, that part of the hypothesis dealing with the lack of ties to the American nation is not upheld. While the emigrants have departed physically from the boundaries of the United States, they are still Americans culturally. They were living in societies within which being American carried considerable prestige. Their reactions to their host societies revolved around American characteristics such as a commitment to a strong work ethic, efficiency, and a high standard for equipment and sanitary conditions.

Both groups of migrants were interested in social and political changes occurring back in the United States. Both groups of migrants customarily retained American citizenship. Both groups of migrants had been good citizens when living in the United States and, now, rarely were they alienated expatriates. In fact, they were much nearer to being American "cultural missionaries."

Despite the differences in their migration motivations, these two groups of American migrants went through very similar processes of adjustments to and absorption in their new societies (or failures in adjustments and absorption). First of all, the multiple, necessary adjustments took time. The pace was almost not noticed. Yet, after a number of years, "staying" migrants suddenly realized just how absorbed they had become.

Via the necessary day-by-day process, these staying migrants developed a sizable, and socially satisfactory, set of acquaintances, friends, and new relatives by marriage. They acquired interesting occupations that afforded enough income to maintain a satisfactory living standard. Their children became "proper products" of their new countries. They felt confident about remaining and recognized how much their social outlooks had evolved since their arrival in either Australia or Israel.

This slow and tenuous process of adjustment-absorption was readily blocked. Migrants could fail to form socially satisfactory networks, or their economic activities might not be rewarding, or perhaps fail to yield an adequate (to them) living standard. Lacking an initial commitment to settle, many would grow impatient to go back. Then, a decision would be made to return to the United States and, hopefully, a more satisfactory life.

Another clear characteristic of these modern migration streams was the extent to which they can be oscillatory. This is especially so for the migrants to Israel. Israel is much nearer to the United States than Australia; hence, it is less expensive to fly there. Also, the various organizations in the American Jewish community constantly sponsor, even subsidize upon occasion, tours to Israel. Hence, a sizable percentage of American migrants have been to Israel one or more times, sometimes for as long as a year, before migrating.

One can migrate to Israel and then decide that more U.S. education or occupational training is needed. One can decide more money is needed to buy a satisfactory apartment in Israel that can only be obtained by returning to work for a number of years in the United States. After such plans are accomplished, there can be a return to Israel. Sometimes, a family can migrate to Israel and then return to the United States. A number of years later, one of the children of such a family may well decide to return to Israel. Indeed, many returned Olim expressed a desire to return to Israel at a future date.

In Chapter 2, reference was made to Gerstein's assertion that Durkheim's *Suicide* (1951) contained a theory about individuals and their linkages to society. In this context, the rate of emigration was viewed as a function of the degree of integration in society from a sociological point of view. In social psychological terms, this translates into the notion that individuals who are less integrated into society are more likely to emigrate. Similarly, Durkheim, in trying to understand the presumptive modes of suicide (1951, p. 148), concluded "that there are not one but various forms of suicide" (p. 277). Thus, it might be argued likewise about emigration.

Durkheim distinguished between "egoistic suicide," with its emphasis on self-involvement and preoccupation, and "altruistic suicide," with its focus on other-orientation and obligation. Similarly, it may be reasonable to speak of "egoistic emigration," as characterizing the self-oriented motives of Yanks moving to Australia, and "altruistic emigration," as describing the motives of Olim moving to Israel. Both were driven by self-expressive motives: the Yanks toward travel and adventure and the Olim toward greater religioethnic self-fulfillments.[1] The Yanks represented the individualized adventurers, for the most part, who were wandering about in the "Anglo world." Olim were ideologists seeking religioethnic experiences in the "Jewish world." Future research should seek to explore further appropriate distinctions among voluntary international migrants in the developed world with respect to their motivations, adjustments, and possible return.

These basic differences were clearly brought out by the ways the Yank "settlers" and Olim "stayers" reacted to their host societies. The settlers, in effect, disappeared inside Australian society. They formed no collective voluntary associations; they seldom had other settlers as friends; and they did not seek out one another.

Most American stayers in Israel did the opposite. They formed collective voluntary associations, such as the Association of Americans and Canadians in Israel (AACI) or joined American-style non-Orthodox synagogues. They often related to overall Israeli society like members of an ethnic group. Yet, this ought to be no surprise, for many Americans in Israel grew up in highly identified sectors of the American Jewish community. Now, they were merely relating to Israeli society as the American Jewish community related to the overall American society.

Not only were these American Jews in Israel concerned about Israeli organizational efficiency, but they also carried over concern about historic American Jewish core values, for example, religious pluralism, tolerance, civil liberties, and civil rights. Some of them expressed these concerns in organized group endeavors. Indeed, Waxman (1989, pp. 150–168) found that even among American Olim in the "Territories" (referred to by some as the West Bank and by others as Judea and Samaria), commonly thought to be right-wing nationalists, liberal political and social values prevailed.

---

[1]Similarly, it may be possible to characterize American emigrants to Canada as "anomic." Just as Durkheim viewed anomic suicide as driven by economic conditions, so it may be argued that "anomic emigration" is motivated by economic elements. While this study did not consider the details of the Canadian case of American emigration, it is likely that financial factors play an important role in motivating such migration.

CONTEMPORARY TRENDS IN MODERN INTERNATIONAL MIGRATION IN THE DEVELOPED WORLD

It is reasonable to conclude that the modernized nations of the world will continue to furnish "modern" migrants. Most of these migrants will be adventurers, such as American sojourners in Australia, who will seek interesting, stimulating experiences in other modern countries with compatible cultures and expect to return to America. These can be English-speaking people going to Canada, Australia, or New Zealand; French-speaking people going to Quebec; Spanish-speaking people to various parts of South America (or, perhaps, southern Florida or California).

A smaller group of these modern migrants will be those seeking to enrich their religious and/or ethnic experiences. These can be people such as Mexican-Americans going to live in Mexico, Americans of Greek descent going to live in Greece, Irish-Americans going to live in Ireland, and so forth. Most of these migrants will return to the United States after a number of years abroad. Others will stay in their new host countries and gradually move into the population like American settlers in Australia. Others will form one-generation, "semiethnic" groups, such as Americans in Israel.

This term, "semiethnic" groups, is used to account for the rapid assimilation into Israeli life of the Israel-born children of American migrants. The organizations formed by Americans in Israel were not aimed at perpetuating an "American Jewish" subgroup in Israel from generation to generation. Rather, these Olim thought it quite desirable that their children be full-fledged Israelis. (The exception might be their frequent efforts to teach their children good English for its international communications value in the modern world.) American-derived organizations, such as the Israeli Reform religious movement, quickly seek to attract as many Israelis of different backgrounds as possible.

Modern migrants will become full-fledged religioethnic groups only when they live in a relatively "incompatible" society. Yet, given the characteristics of this modern migration, this should be a rare event. For example, some American Protestants go to live in Israel for religious reasons. There they live in their own subgroups, attend their own Christian churches (in the midst of Jewish and Muslim dominating cultural groups), and want their children to grow up to be believing Protestants who marry other Protestants.

On the basis of this study a number of propositions emerge that deal with emigrants in the developed world:

1. Even countries that receive immigrants are still producing emigrants from their native population.
2. American and other emigrants in the developed world will continue to move abroad to seek the "new frontier" driven by motives of adventure,

travel, and to a lesser extent ideology. The compatibility of economic and educational institutions, technology, and cultures will encourage this pattern.

3. Their adjustments will be proportional to the differences in culture between the receiving and sending societies. Adjustments to cultural and material conditions will be eased by satisfying social integration (usually facilitated by higher-than-average incomes and education) and will be exacerbated in their absence. Americans intending to return may not even acknowledge adjustment problems and going home may not be related to such problems.

4. Among American emigrants only a minority will remain abroad over the long haul. For those Americans who remain, behavioral assimilation will be fairly rapid and occur within one generation. However, American identity symbolized by retention of citizenship and English in non-Anglo countries will persist into the second generation.

If these propositions are further substantiated by subsequent additional research, then it behooves the developed nations of the world to consider the following policies:

1. Create government bodies to analyze the consequences for its society of emigration of its citizens as well as the immigration of aliens. This seems more important where a "brain drain" emigration seems to be large scale.

2. Develop policies that respond appropriately to short-term as opposed to long-term migrants, as many migrants may only be in the host country for a few years.

3. Create opportunities for the new emigrants to share the cultural insights and social skills of their former society that might enrich the host society, as for example the concerns of Americans for environmental protection, civil rights and liberties, and religious pluralism.

4. Recognize that government policy is limited in its ability to influence decisions to settle. Integration into society is largely dependent on satisfying friendship, family, and occupational relationships. Such strategies as assisted passage or immigrant rights and benefits may be useful to stimulate selective migration (for critical skills, for instance). However, most migrants will not settle after their contractual obligations end. Americans who genuinely want to settle will usually have enough money to do so on their own. Thus, government assistance programs may encourage temporary movement of voluntary international migrants to their countries, but not actual settlement.

5. Encourage limited migration or temporary residence with guarantees of

work, assisted passage, and other special benefits. Incentives can influence decisions to remain for limited stretches of a year or two. But any such policy will attract the more adventuresome, not the alienated, and thus will not yield large numbers of settlers. Policies that discourage or "punish" integration (such as refusal to recognize American or other educational credentials) will certainly discourage settlement.

6. Deter efforts to force migrants to change citizenship or otherwise make a permanent, formal commitment to one society or another. Few will surrender their citizenship, and they see no reason why they cannot live abroad for 20 years or longer while still retaining their status, particularly if they are American citizens.

Return migration does not mean rejection or dissatisfaction with the new society. The nature of this migrant phenomenon is that people are always in the process of deciding to stay longer, rather than making a final decision to settle. Being affluent, these migrants do not feel stranded or irrevocably committed, do not feel cut off from their homeland, and frequently intended to return at any rate. Retention of such migrants would require government control over social forces that promote integration, and that is largely beyond governmental influence.

SUMMARY

This study sought to investigate the motivations for migration, adjustments in the host country, and the factors in return migration within a social psychological perspective for Americans moving to Australia and Israel. This study of emigration was carried out at a time when the volume of immigration to the United States was three times greater than the amount of emigration, but the study of the former exceeded by seven times the study of the latter.

The findings from the preceding chapters were reviewed and the dynamics of emigration were identified. This process suggested that self-expressive factors predominated in explaining motivation, self-instrumental elements in accounting for adjustments, and others-expressive dimensions in dealing with the issue of remaining or returning. In addition, some of the theoretical and policy implications of this research were discussed.

The increase in the possibility of the exchange of people from one society to another ultimately can be an enriching experience for both the guests and the hosts. However, the structure of relationships in the new society needs to be conducive to creating social interchange rather than engendering mutual hostility.

As the author of the Book of Proverbs wrote, "Better a neighbor near at hand than a brother far away." This thought was reworded in the modern day by Stephen Vincent Benet, who wrote:

Remember that when you say
"I will have none of this exile and this stranger
For his face is not like my face and his speech is strange,"
You have denied America with that word.

Indeed, neither America nor the other nations can deny any more that emigration is an enduring feature of life in the developed world and, hopefully, all can learn to benefit from it.

References

Ajzen, L., and M. Fishbein. 1980. *Understanding Attitudes and Predicting Social Behavior*. Englewood Cliffs, NJ: Prentice Hall.

Alba, R., and M. B. Chamlin. 1983. "A Preliminary Examination of Ethnic Identification among Whites." *American Sociological Review* 48: 240–247.

Andrews, F., and R. Messenger. 1973. *Multivariate Nominal Scale Analysis*. Ann Arbor, MI: Institute for Social Research, University of Michigan.

Antonovsky, A. 1968. *Americans and Canadians in Israel, Report No. 1 (Rev.)*. Jerusalem, Israel.

Antonovsky, A., and D. Katz. 1979. *From the Golden to the Promised Land*. Darby, PA: Norwood Editions.

Appleyard, R. T. 1962. "Determinants of Return Migration: A Social-Economic Study of United Kingdom Migrants Who Returned from Australia." *The Economic Record* 38: 352–368.

Australian Department of Labour and Immigration. 1969. *Survey of American Settlers*. Canberra: Government Printer.

Australian Department of Labour and Immigration. 1971. *Survey of U.S. Settlers, Phase Two*. Canberra: Government Printer.

Australian Department of Labour and Immigration. 1973. *Australian Immigration, Consolidated Statistics*. Canberra: Australian Government Publishing Service.

Australian Department of Labour and Immigration. 1983. *Australian Immigration Consolidated Statistics*. Canberra: Australian Government Publishing Service.

Avruch, K. 1981. *American Immigrants in Israel: Social Identities and Change*. Chicago: University of Chicago Press.

Babbie, E. 1986. *The Practice of Social Research* (5th ed.). Belmont, CA: Wadsworth Publishing Company.

Bachi, R. 1974. "The Jewish Population." In *Israel Pocket Library: Society*, pp. 1–28. Jerusalem: Keter Publishing.

Bardo, J. W., and D. J. Bardo. 1980a. "Adjustment of American Teachers in Victoria, Australia." *Psychological Reports* 47: 599–608.

Bardo, J. W., and D. J. Bardo. 1980b. "Dimensions of Adjustment for American Settlers in Melbourne, Australia." *Multivariate Experimental Clinical Research* 5: 23–28.

Bardo, J. W., and D. J. Bardo. 1980c. "From Settlers to Migrants: A Symbolic Interactionist Interpretation of American Migration to Australia." *Studies in Symbolic Interaction* 3: 194–232.

Bardo, J. W., and D. J. Bardo. 1980d. "Note on Adjustment of Married American School Teachers in Victoria, Australia." *Psychological Reports* 49: 623–627.

Bardo, J. W., and D. J. Bardo. 1980e. "Sociodemographic Correlates of Adjustment for American Migrants in Australia." *Journal of Social Psychology* 112: 255–260.

Bardo, J. W., and D. J. Bardo. 1981. "American Migrants in Australia: An Exploratory Study of Adjustments." *Sociological Focus* 14: 147–156.

Beijer, G. 1969. "Modern Patterns of International Migratory Movements." In J. A. Jackson (Ed.), *Migration*, pp. 11–59. New York: Cambridge University Press.

Berman, G. S. 1978. "The Work Adjustment of North American Immigrants in Israel." Jerusalem, Israel. Research Report, Work and Welfare Research Institute.

Berman, G. S. 1979. "Why North Americans Migrate to Israel." *Jewish Journal of Sociology* 21: 135–144.

Biernacki, P., and D. Waldorf. 1981. "Snowball Sampling." *Sociological Methods and Research* 10: 141–163.

Blejer, M. I., and I. Goldberg. 1980. "Return Migration-Expectations versus Reality: A Case Study of Western Immigrants to Israel." *Population Economics* 2: 433–449.

Bogue, D. 1961. "Techniques and Hypotheses for the Study of Differential Migration." *International Population Conference* 1961: Paper 114.

Bogue, D. 1969. *Principles of Demography*. New York: Wiley and Sons.

Bovenkerk, F. 1974. *The Sociology of Return Migration: A Bibliographic Essay*. The Hague: Martinus Nijhoff.

Cerase, F. 1967. "A Study of Italian Migrants Returning from the U.S.A." *International Migration Review* 1: 67–74.

Christy, J. 1972. *The Non-Refugees*. Toronto: Peter Martin Associates.

Cohen, S. M. 1988. *Unity and Polarization in Judaism Today: The Attitudes of American and Israeli Jews*. New York: American Jewish Committee.

Comay, Y. 1971. "Determinants of Return Migration: Canadian Professionals in the United States." *Southern Economic Journal* 37: 318–322.

Cuddy, D. 1977. *The Yanks Are Coming: American Migration to Australia*. New York: R&E Associates.

Danet, B., and H. Hartman. 1972. "On Proteksia: Orientations toward the Use of Personal Influence in Israeli Bureaucracy." *Journal of Comparative Administration* 3: 405–434.

Danon, E. 1988. "To Increase Efficiency and to Fire." *Maariv* (February 23): 17 (Hebrew).

Dashefsky, A. (Ed.). 1976. *Ethnic Identity in Society*. Chicago: Rand McNally.

Dashefsky, A., and B. Lazerwitz. 1983. "The Role of Religious Identification in North American Migration to Israel." *Journal for the Scientific Study of Religion* 22: 263–275.

Dashefsky, A., and B. Lazerwitz. 1986. "North American Migration to Israel: Stayers and Leavers." *Contemporary Jewry* 7: 44–63.

Dashefsky, A., J. DeAmicis, and B. Lazerwitz. 1984. "American Emigration: Similarities and Differences among Migrants to Australia and Israel." *Comparative Social Research* 7: 337–347.

DeAmicis, J. 1980. Review of *The Yanks Are Coming: American Migration to Australia* by Dennis Cuddy. *International Migration Review* 14: 268.

Durkheim, E. 1951. *Suicide*. Translated by J. A. Spaulding and G. Simpson. Glencoe, IL: Free Press. (Originally published in 1897.)

Eisenstadt, S. N. 1954. *The Absorption of Immigrants*. London: Routledge & Kegan Paul.

Elizur, D. 1974. "The Long Way Back." In *Jewish Agency Annual*, pp. 114–125. Jerusalem: Office for Economic and Social Research, Jewish Agency.

Elizur, D. 1979. "Israelis in the United States: Motives, Attitudes, and Intentions." *American Jewish Yearbook* 80: 53–67.

Engel, G. 1970. "North American Settlers in Israel." *American Jewish Yearbook* 71: 161–187.

Evans, M. D. R. 1984. "Immigrant Women in Australia: Resources, Family, and Work." *International Migration Review* 18: 1063–1090.

Finifter, A. 1976. "American Emigration." *Society* 13: 30–42.

Finifter, A., and B. M. Finifiter. 1980a. "Report to Respondents: Survey of Americans in Australia." Private publication prepared at Michigan State University, East Lansing.

Finifter, A., and B. M. Finifter. 1980b. "Citizenship Decision-Making: Durability and Change of National Allegiance and Identification among American Migrants in Australia." Paper presented at the Annual Meeting of the American Political Science Association, Washington, August.

Finifter, A., and B. M. Finifter. 1982. "Values and Migration Decisions: How Personal Values Affect Perceived Life Opportunities and National Commitments of American Migrants in Australia." Paper presented at Annual Meeting of the American Sociological Association, San Francisco, September.

Finifter, A.W., and B. M. Finifter. 1989. "Party Identification and Political Adaptation of American Migrants in Australia." *Journal of Politics* 51: 599–629.

Gerstein, D. R. 1983. "Durkheim's Paradigm Reconstructing a Social Theory." In R. Collins (Ed.), *Sociological Theory*, pp. 234–258. San Francisco: Jossey-Bass.

Gitelman, Z. 1982. *Becoming Israeli: Political Resocialization of Soviet and American Immigrants.* New York: Praeger.

Goldberg, A. I. 1985. "A New Look at Aliyah Influences among North American Jews." *The Jewish Journal of Sociology* 27: 81–102.

Goldscheider, C. 1971. *Population, Modernization, and Social Structure.* Boston: Little Brown.

Goldscheider, C. 1974. "American Aliya: Sociological and Demographic Perspectives." In Marshall Sklare (Ed.), *The Jew in American Society*, pp. 337–384. New York: Behrman.

Grove, L. 1987. "In *Full Metal Jacket*, Kubrick Just Wanted to Tell a Good Story." *Hartford Courant*, July 12, G1, G5.

Haour-Knipe, M. 1990. "Deciding to Move Abroad: Juggling Family and Career." Paper presented at the Annual Meeting of the Society for Applied Anthropology, University of York, March.

Heckelman, A. J. 1974. *American Volunteers and Israel's War of Independence.* New York: Ktav.

Heiss, J. 1969. "Factors Related to Immigrant Assimilation: Pre-Migration Traits." *Social Forces* 47: 422–428.

Herman, S. W. 1970. *American Students in Israel.* Ithaca: Cornell University Press.

Historical Statistics of the United States, 1975.

Homans, G. C. 1964. "Bringing Men Back In." *American Sociological Review* 29: 809–818.

Houstoun, M. F., R. G. Kramer, and J. M. Barrett. 1984. "Female Predominance of Immigration to the United States since 1930: A First Look." *International Migration Review* 18: 908–963.

Hvidt, K. 1975. *Flight to America.* New York: Academic Press.

Immigration Advisory Council Committee on Social Patterns. 1973. *Inquiry into the Departure of Settlers from Australia, Final Report, July 1973.* Canberra: Australian Government Publishing Service.

Isaacs, H. 1966. *American Jews in Israel.* New York: John Day.

Jackson, J. A. (Ed.) 1969. *Migration.* New York: Cambridge University Press.

Jansen, C. 1969. "Some Sociological Aspects of Migration." In J. A. Jackson (Ed.), *Migration*, pp. 60–73. New York: Cambridge University Press.

Jubas, H. 1974. *The Adjustment Process of Americans and Canadians in Israel and Their Integration into Israeli Society.* Doctoral dissertation, Michigan State University.

Kaufmann, S. 1987. *American Immigrants in Israel: A Selected Annotated Bibliography 1948–85.* New York: American Jewish Committee.

Kohn, M. L. 1987. "Cross-National Research as an Analytic Strategy." *American Sociological Review* 52: 713–731.

Lantz, J. C. 1987. *Cumulative Index of Sociology Journals 1971–1985.* Washington, D.C.: The American Sociological Association.

Lapide, P. E. 1961. *A Century of U. S. Aliya*. Jerusalem: The Association of Americans and Canadians in Israel.

Lazerwitz, B., and M. Harrison. 1980. "Comparison of Denominational Identification and Membership." *Journal for the Scientific Study of Religion* 19: 361–367.

Lee, E. 1966. "A Theory of Migration." *Demography* 3: 47–57.

Lewin, K. 1936. *Principles of Topological Psychology*. New York: McGraw Hill.

Lewin, K. 1951. *Field Theory in Social Science*. Edited by D. Cartwright. New York: Harper & Row.

Liebman, C. 1988. "Conceptions of 'State of Israel' in Israeli Society." *The Jerusalem Quarterly* 47: 95–107.

Lukomskyj, O., and P. Richards. 1986. "Return Migration from Australia, A Case Study." *International Migration* 24: 603–632.

Matras, J. 1973. *Population and Societies*. Englewood Cliffs, NJ: Prentice-Hall.

Meyer, M., C. Robinson, and J. Gordon. 1988. "Capitalism's Last Frontier." *Newsweek*, May 16, p. 52.

Newman, W. M. 1973. *American Pluralism*. New York: Harper & Row.

Petersen, W. 1975. *Population* (3rd ed.). New York: Macmillan.

Petersen, W. 1970. "A General Typology of Migration." In C. J. Jansen (Ed.), *Readings in the Sociology of Migration*, pp. 49–68. Oxford: Pergamon.

Richmond, A. 1967. *Postwar Immigrants to Canada*. Toronto: University of Toronto Press.

Richmond, A. 1968. "Return Migration from Canada to Britain." *Population Studies* 22: 263–271.

Rose, A. M. 1969. *Migrants in Europe*. Minneapolis: University of Minnesota Press.

Rossi, P. H. 1955. *Why Families Move: A Study in the Social Psychology of Residential Mobility*. Glencoe, IL: Free Press.

Scott, W. A., and R. Scott. 1989. *Adaptation of Immigrants*. Oxford: Pergamon.

Sobel, Z. 1985. *Migrants from the Promised Land*. New Brunswick, NJ: Transaction Books.

Sonquist, J., E. Baker, and J. Morgan. 1971. *Searching for Structure Alias AID III*. Ann Arbor, MI: Institute for Social Research, University of Michigan.

Stouffer, S. A. 1940. "Intervening Opportunities: A Theory Relating Mobility and Distance." *American Sociological Review* 5: 845–867.

Tabory, E. 1975. *Motivation for Migration: A Comparative Study of American and Soviet Academic Immigrants to Israel*. M.A. thesis, Bar Ilan University.

Tabory, E. 1988/1989. "An Attempt to Cope with Children's Migration: Parents of American Immigrants to Israel." *Israel Social Science Research* 6: 40–51.

Tabory, E., and B. Lazerwitz. 1983. "Americans in the Israeli Reform and Conservative Denominations: Religiosity under an Ethnic Shield?" *Review of Religious Research* 24: 177–187.

Thomas, W. I., and Znaniecki, F. 1920. *The Polish Peasant in Europe and America*. Chicago: University of Chicago Press.

United Nations Demographic Yearbook, 1977. 1978. New York: United Nations.

U.S. Bureau of the Census. 1975. *Historical Statistics of the United States, Colonial Times to 1970*. Washington: U.S. Government Printing Office.

Warren, R., and Kraly, E. P. 1985. "The Elusive Exodus: Emigration from the United States." *Population Trends and Public Policy* 8: 1–17.

Waxman, C. 1989. *American Aliya*. Detroit: Wayne State University Press.

Waxman, C., and Appel, M. 1986. *To Israel and Back*. New York: American Jewish Committee.

Zinger, Z. 1974. "State of Israel." In *Israel Pocket Library: Immigration and Settlement*, pp. 50–74. Jerusalem: Keter Publishing.

Author Index

Subject Index

Absorption, 13, 78, 79–80, 81–82, 92–93, 110, 113, 114–115, 128–131, 148
Absorption center, 87–88
Adjustment, 13, 77, 79–81, 82, 84–93, 98–99, 127, 146
Adjustment challenge
  expressive, 81–82
  instrumental, 81–82
Alienation, 19, 32, 42–45, 47, 49–50
Aliya, 35
Altruistic, 120, 152
Americans
  alienated, 12, 30–32, 42–45, 47, 49–50, 71–72, 134, 146
  in Australia (the Yanks), 25–26, 29–31, 33, 35, 36–46, 53–54, 55–60, 61–65, 71–72, 76–77, 83–88, 90, 93–96, 98–99, 112, 140–141, 145–146, 148, 150–151
  in Canada, 29–31, 33, 145
  characteristics, 4–5, 21, 33, 38, 59, 76, 77, 80–81, 84, 85, 91–93, 138, 150–151
  citizenship, 113, 127, 132–137, 140–141, 148–150. *See also* Dual citizenship
  contract workers, 57–60, 128–129
  emigrants, 5, 12, 16–18, 23n, 32–33, 47n, 53–54
  explanations, 6, 32–33, 53, 71–72, 99, 144, 146, 147, 148
  identity, 138, 139, 150
  impact, 113, 148, 150, 152–153
  integration, 19–20, 60, 92–93, 94–95, 121, 138, 149, 151. *See also* Integration

Americans (*Cont.*)
  in Israel (the Olim), 27–28, 29–31, 33, 35, 36–40, 46–54, 47n, 60–61, 63, 65–66, 67–68, 71–72, 77–81, 87–89, 91–93, 95–96, 98–99, 112, 138, 141, 145–146, 148, 150–151
  leavers. *See* Leavers
  motivations, 35–36, 40–41, 53–54, 60, 69, 71–72, 77, 93
  Olim. *See* Americans in Israel
  returning to America. *See* American similarities; Leavers; Migration-cycle; Migration-return; Reentering America; Sojourners
  settlers. *See* Settlers
  similarities, 101–103, 112, 113–114, 115, 119–120, 145–146
  sojourners. *See* Sojourners
  status of, 38, 80–81, 98
  stayers. *See* Stayers
  undergraduates, 10
  Yanks. *See* Americans in Australia
Anglo-ethnic, 77, 80, 92, 93, 111, 152, 153
Anomic, 152n
Assimilation. *See* Americans-integration; Integration
Australia
  business, 83
  characteristics, 74–77, 86, 90
  contract workers, 57–58
  data sources, 22n, 23n, 22–23, 33
  efficiency, 38, 77–78, 83, 90, 99, 148
  immigrants, 21, 25–26, 75–76
  information on, 74

163